THE CANADIANS IN BRITAIN

1939—1944

28292—1

THE decision to publish a series of contemporary historical booklets on the Canadian Army was taken by the Minister of National Defence the Honourable J. L. Ralston, C.M.G., D.S.O., in February 1944. The text of the present booklet was compiled and written by the Historical Section of the General Staff, Canadian Military Headquarters in Great Britain, and was completed in October 1944.

Some passages from articles contributed to the *Canadian Geographical Journal* by members of the Section have been incorporated, by permission of the Canadian Geographical Society.

The illustrations consist mainly of paintings by official War Artists of the Canadian Army and photographs by Canadian Army Overseas Film and Photo Units.

THE CANADIAN ARMY AT WAR

The Canadians in Britain

1939-1944

With a Foreword by
Lieutenant-General J. C. MURCHIE, C.B., C.B.E.
Chief of the General Staff, Canada

Published by Authority of the Minister of National Defence

PRINTED BY THE KING'S PRINTER AT OTTAWA, CANADA

FOREWORD

This booklet is the first of a series, compiled from official records, which is being produced with the object of giving the people of Canada somewhat fuller information than it has hitherto been possible to publish concerning the work of their Army in the present war.

This first volume is concerned with the experiences and activities of the Canadians in the United Kingdom during the long and trying years of waiting which preceded their becoming engaged in active operations. Later booklets will tell how they acquitted themselves when action came.

The story which the present volume relates is unique in the history of the Empire. It describes in detail the important role which Canadian troops played in the defence of Britain, in the days when that country was threatened with invasion. It tells also the story of the troops' relations with their British hosts. More than a quarter of a million Canadian volunteers, who had enlisted in the hope of seeing early action, were stationed in the Mother Country, without being given the opportunity of a blow at the enemy, for periods of up to five years. The maintenance—and, indeed, the improvement—of their morale and discipline, under these singularly difficult conditions, reflects the greatest credit on two parties: the brave, generous and hospitable people of Britain, on one side, and the officers and men of the Canadian Army Overseas on the other. The whole incident is one which hosts and guests alike will remember with pride in times to come; and it will have its effect—and a very desirable effect—upon the future of the British Commonwealth. The Commonwealth is based upon mutual goodwill and understanding; and those qualities have never been better exemplified than in the relations of Canadian and Briton during the years treated in this little book.

J. C. Murchie

Lieutenant-General,
Chief of the General Staff.

THE CANADIANS IN BRITAIN
1939—1944

I. Five Years in Britain

The Canadians Arrive—Warders in the Gate—Sussex by the Sea—"Scene: England; Afterwards France".

II. The Weapon on the Anvil

The Shadow of Invasion—The Battle Drill Idea—The Prelude to Attack.

III. The Days of the Blitz

A Grand-Stand View—"A Dreadful and Impassioned Drama"—A Big Week in Liverpool—Hit-and-Run.

IV. Sappers at Work

Drilling and Tunnelling—Barring the Gates—The Road Builders—Harnessing the Waters—To Keep Them Flying—The Quest for Strategic Minerals—The Constructors.

V. A Little Behind the Front

The Reinforcement Units—Scottish Forests and Canadian Foresters—Under the Geneva Cross—Young Ladies in Khaki.

VI. The Canadians and the British People

Getting to Know Each Other—"Single Men in Barracks"—A Quarter of a Million Ambassadors.

I

FIVE YEARS IN BRITAIN

ON the 17th of December, 1939, a convoy of great ships steamed into the River Clyde. They were liners whose names were household words: *Aquitania, Empress of Britain, Empress of Australia, Duchess of Bedford, Monarch of Bermuda;* and they were escorted by famous vessels of the Royal Navy—the battle-cruiser *Repulse,* the battleship *Resolution,* the aircraft-carrier *Furious,* and several smaller vessels, among which were four Canadian destroyers.

The Clydesiders who saw this great armada sailing up their river had no fore-knowledge of its coming, nor did they know whom it might carry. Their first thought was that it bore men of the British Expeditionary Force returning from France for Christmas leave. Soon, however, they were undeceived. From the crowded transports came the voices of soldiers, loudly and unmistakably proclaiming their origin. They "spelt out in unison 'C-A-N-A-D-A' and concluded on a mighty crescendo 'Canada!'". The 1st Canadian Division was arriving.

Thus began one of the most remarkable episodes in the history of the British Empire. The 7,500 men who arrived in the United Kingdom that winter day were the vanguard of more than 335,000 Canadian soldiers whom the war was to bring thither during the next five years. Although nobody expected it in 1939, most of these men were to spend the greater part of those years in Britain. An army of volunteers enlisted in the expectation of very early active service, they found themselves committed instead to a defensive and largely static role for years to come. Not until the Allied invasions of Sicily and Italy in 1943 and France a year later did the Canadians find themselves engaged in such great and protracted operations against the enemy as they had believed to be imminent in 1939.

This little book attempts to tell the story of the great body of Canadians who thus took up an habitation enforced in the British Isles during the years 1939-44. It is a tale not without significance. Canadians of the future, it is true, will doubtless find the chief interest of this Second World War in their countryman's share in the campaigns in Italy and in France, and in the other theatres where they have played or will yet play their parts. Nevertheless, they will be well advised to spare a glance for the remarkable spectacle of the transplantation of a quarter of a million young men (and women) for five years from the New World to England, and the story of their life and doings there. It is an incident which will have its due effect upon the future of Canada and the British Commonwealth, and their place in the world.

THE CANADIANS ARRIVE

The "First Flight" of the 1st Canadian Division were not the very earliest Canadian soldiers to reach the United Kingdom in the Second World War. A few individuals, indeed, were actually serving there when war broke out. One such was Lt.-Col. E. L. M. Burns (later Lieutenant-General Commanding the Canadian Corps in Italy), who was attending the Imperial Defence College and was immediately seized upon by the High Commissioner for Canada to assist him in dealing with the innumerable military problems which descended upon Canada House at the declaration of war. On 27 October, 1939, another distinguished soldier, Brigadier H. D. G. Crerar (subsequently General and G.O.C.-in-C. First Canadian Army) landed in the United Kingdom to establish the nucleus of a Canadian Mili-

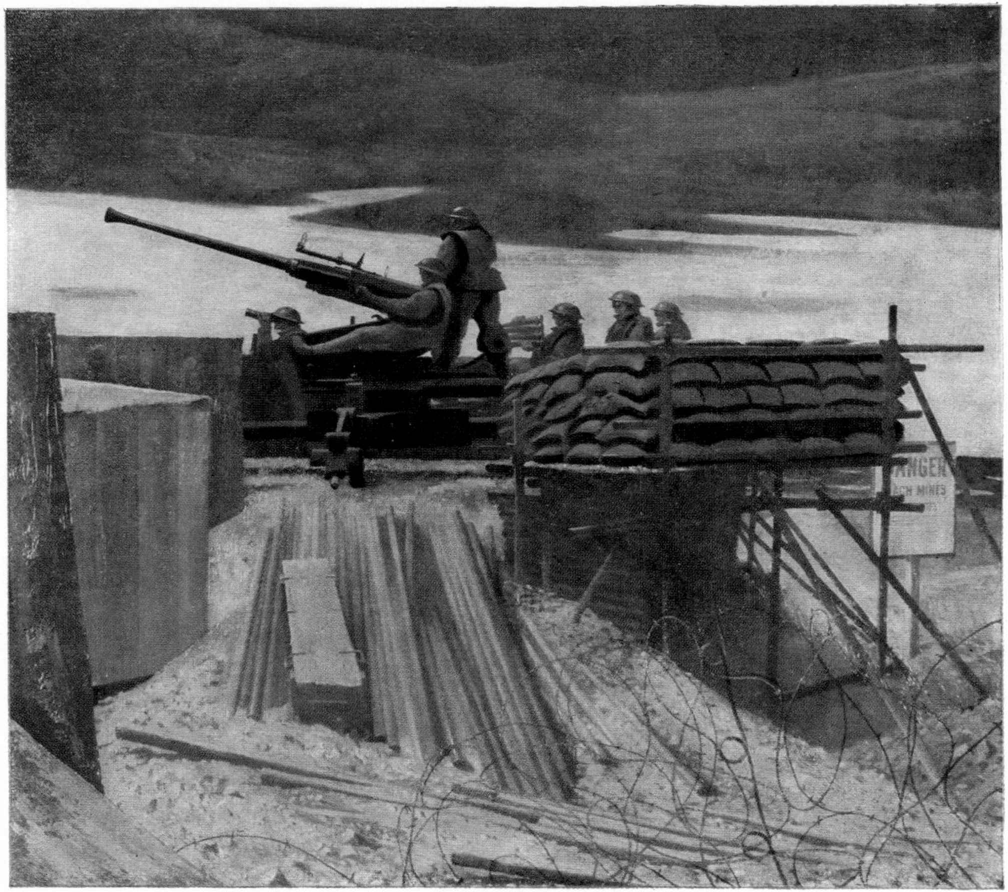

From an oil painting by Major C. F. Comfort.

DAWN ALERT

(Southern England, 1943)

tary Headquarters in London. This Headquarters was already functioning in Cockspur Street when the 1st Canadian Division, commanded by Major-General (later General) A. G. L. McNaughton, arrived on British soil.

The First Flight was followed, before the end of the year, by a Second Flight comprising the balance of the 1st Division. It arrived on 30 December. On 7 February 1940 the transports of a Third Flight dropped anchor in British waters. This was composed mainly of "ancillary troops", including large numbers of artillery, designed as the Canadian contribution to the "Corps Troops" of a British Corps of which, it was expected, the 1st Canadian Division would, at least temporarily, form a part. Thus before the winter ended the initial program for the despatch of Canadian troops to Britain was complete. The strength of the Canadian Active Service Force in the United Kingdom was about 23,000 all ranks.

This was only the beginning. Early in 1940 the Canadian Government announced its intention of sending the 2nd Canadian Division overseas, and in the course of that year the units of the Division, commanded by Major-General V. W. Odlum, landed in the United Kingdom from a succession of convoys. The main contingents disembarked on 2 August and 5 September, walking straight into the fury of Goering's first great air attacks on England; but the last infantry battalions did not arrive until Christmas Day. Some units of the Division (including two battalions of infantry) arrived in England not direct from Canada, but from Iceland, where they had spent several bleak months in garrison.

With the 2nd Division concentrated in Britain, the formation of an independent Canadian Corps became practicable, and such a Corps—the heir of the traditions of the Canadian Corps of the last war—came into existence on the same Christmas Day which witnessed the arrival of the last of the 2nd Division's battalions from Canada. The New Year of 1941 found more than 56,000 Canadian soldiers in the United Kingdom.

Britain was now a beleaguered fortress. France had for the moment been driven out of the war, and the coast of Europe was in enemy hands from the North Cape to the Pyrenees. In these circumstances the Dominion of Canada, determined to strengthen to the utmost the defence of the heart of the Commonwealth and the last European foothold of freedom, continued to pour troops across the Atlantic. During the critical days of the summer of 1940 the 3rd and subsequently the 4th Canadian Divisions had been mobilized in Canada. In July of 1941 the main body of the 3rd Division, which was commanded by Major-General C. B. Price, arrived to join the force in Britain.

While it thus grew steadily in size, the Canadian field force was becoming more formidable in other respects. Until now it had been primarily an infantry force of the traditional type, with virtually no armoured component. During 1941 the picture in this respect changed rapidly. The first Canadian armoured formation to appear in Britain was the 1st Canadian Army Tank Brigade, commanded by Brigadier (later Major-General) F. F. Worthington, which landed in June. A still more important one arrived in October and November, when the 5th Canadian Armoured Division (which had earlier been designated the 1st Canadian Armoured Division) disembarked. Its commander was Major-General (later Lieutenant-General) E. W. Sansom. By the end of 1941 the number of Canadian soldiers in Britain was nearly 125,000.

The force was still far from complete. The last Canadian division to reach England was the 4th Canadian Armoured Division, which arrived in the autumn of 1942 under Major-General Worthington, who had returned to Canada to take command of it. The provision of a second Army Tank Brigade thereafter completed the picture as far as major formations were concerned; but a full catalogue of the field army—to say nothing of the numerous static units—contains in addition to these a vast variety of Corps, Army, G.H.Q. and Lines of Communication troops, amounting in the aggregate to many thousands, each unit with its essential function. As additional units to complete the Canadian order of battle arrived in the United Kingdom, the Canadian strength there continued to increase. It finally reached its peak in the early autumn of 1943, at a time when a considerable force of Canadians had already left England for the Mediterranean area, but before the departure of the balance of the 1st Canadian Corps. By this time Canada's contribution to the Army of Liberation which was to cross the Channel in the summer of 1944 was virtually complete; there were now rather more than 200,000 of her soldiers in the British Isles alone. With the despatch of additional troops to Italy that autumn, the strength in the United Kingdom was somewhat reduced.

The field force had long outgrown the control of a single Corps Headquarters. On 6 April, 1942, in consequence, Headquarters, First Canadian Army, had come into existence with General McNaughton as G.O.C.-in-C. General Crerar returned from Canada, where he had been Chief of the General Staff since the summer of 1940, to succeed General McNaughton in the command of the Canadian Corps, which now became the 1st Canadian Corps. Headquarters, 2nd Canadian Corps, was set up on 15 January, 1943, with General Sansom as Corps Commander; and the two Corps "fought" together in the following March in the manoeuvres known as Exercise "Spartan".

* * * *

At the time when the Canadian Army was finally committed to action in its two European theatres in 1944, its total overseas strength was more than a quarter of a million officers and men; and every one of these had been brought from Canada to the United Kingdom across waters which the Germans had claimed were controlled by their submarines and aircraft. It is a remarkable fact, and one rather too easily forgotten, that this tremendous movement of troops has gone on, over a period of five years, with no effective interference whatever from the enemy.

The actual total of Canadian soldiers lost at sea while en route from Canada to the United Kingdom is 73 all ranks. All of these men were lost in the sinking of one small vessel, the ss. *Nerissa.* This ship, which was not part of a troop convoy but was sailing independently, with some Canadian troops among her passengers, fell victim to an enemy submarine on the night of 30 April, 1941, when some 120 miles off Northern Ireland. The ship was struck by three torpedoes and sank in about four minutes. Thirty-five Canadian army personnel survived and were picked up by British destroyers.

This tragic but unique exception serves merely to call attention to the remarkably efficient organization of the protection of troops on the trans-Atlantic route. The magnitude of the task staggers the imagination; the magnitude of the triumph is no less. To the Royal Navy, the Royal Canadian Navy, the United States Navy, the French Navy and the Polish Navy, to the Royal Air Force and the Royal Canadian Air Force, and to the men of the Merchant Navies, must go in full measure the credit for a truly extraordinary achievement.

During the early part of the war, Canadian troops were brought to Britain mainly in convoys of liners like that which brought the First Flight. This continued to be the case through 1942, though by that year a convoy of more than three transports was exceptional. The largest number of men reaching the United Kingdom in one convoy was just a little less than 14,000, on Troop Convoy No. 15. This eight-ship convoy brought the main body of the 5th Canadian Armoured Division into British ports in November, 1941.

HALIFAX, DECEMBER, 1939

Men of the 1st Canadian Division embarking for the great adventure.

THE CANADIANS ARRIVE

The "First Flight" of the 1st Canadian Division lands in Scotland, 17th December, 1939.

Photo by Keystone Press Agency

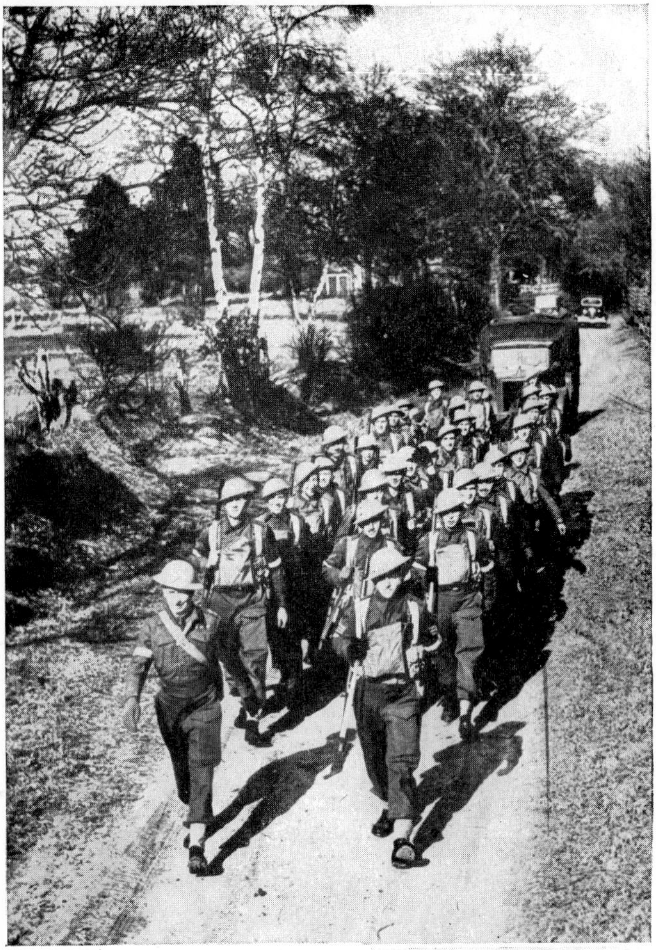

ENGLISH SPRING, 1940

Canadian troops swinging through the southern countryside.

ALDERSHOT, JUNE, 1940

Their Majesties visiting the Toronto Scottish while the Canadians were under orders for France.

During the latter part of 1942, the practice began of employing, instead of convoys of several ships, single vessels of exceptional size and speed, capable of crossing the Atlantic in a very short time and of carrying as many men as a whole convoy of vessels of more moderate tonnage. During 1942-43 the largest liners in the world, the *Queen Mary* and *Queen Elizabeth*, carried vast numbers of Canadian troops across the Atlantic.

Such was the growth of the Canadian Army Overseas, which gradually, over a period of four years, developed from one raw infantry division, armed mainly with the weapons of the last war, into an army of five divisions, equipped in the most modern manner, and trained in the light of this war's experience until it was the best-trained army the Dominion had ever possessed. Of this training, more later; for the moment, our task is to sketch the successive changes which events produced in the role of the Canadians while the field army remained in the island fortress.

WARDERS IN THE GATE

The first Canadians reached England during the period which a contemporary diplomat called the "phony war": the months separating the brief and brutal campaign in September, 1939, which saw the destruction of Poland, from the scarcely longer campaigns in the spring of 1940 in which the Germans overran Norway, Holland and Belgium and struck down France. During those months the 1st Canadian Division was training in England and looking forward to taking its place with the B.E.F. then in France. Its complement of motor transport was still uncompleted when the storm broke in the West and Britain found herself confronting the most desperate crisis in her modern history.

To many a Canadian it is and long will be a source of quiet pride that in the dark time which followed men from Canada shared the perils of the British people and guarded with them the last redoubt of European freedom; that in that crisis the 1st Canadian Division was one of the firm pivots upon which rested the defence of Britain, and a solid symbol of the unity of the Empire in those days when the Empire stood alone.

The story of the various projects for the employment of Canadian troops on the Continent at this period may later be told in detail elsewhere. In this account of the Canadians in Britain, space can be found for only the briefest outline of them.

The advent of the eventful spring of 1940 found the Canadians at Aldershot, training hard. It was on 9 April that the Germans struck at Norway. Within a few days the War Office turned to General McNaughton for troops to assist in the campaign which it was necessary to improvise in that country. As a result, a special Canadian assault force of 1,300 men was very rapidly organized from the 1st Division with a view to participating in the projected attack on Trondhjem. It moved to Scotland, where it awaited orders to embark which never came. The Trondhjem operation was cancelled; and the assault force returned to Aldershot. This was the Canadians' first disappointment that year. It was far from being the last.

On the heels of the Norwegian crisis came the Battle of the Low Countries. On 10 May the Germans broke into Belgium and Holland, and within a few days the British and French Armies in the field were in desperate straits. By 22 May the Germans were sweeping up the Channel coast, while the British Expeditionary Force was falling back on Dunkirk, and the question in every mind was whether any important part of it could be saved from destruction. In these circumstances it was natural that the 1st Canadian Division, one of the very few formations in Britain then in an advanced state of training, should once more become an immediate element in British military calculations.

On 23 May General McNaughton was informed by the War Office that it was proposed to entrust to him the command of a force charged with the task of restoring the com-

PLYMOUTH, JUNE, 1940

Canadians of the forlorn hope embark for France.

⁂ ⁂ ⁂

ALDERSHOT, APRIL, 1940

Under cover of darkness, Canadian troops intended for the Norwegian Expedition march to the station to entrain.

munications of the B.E.F. with the Channel ports of Boulogne and Calais. That evening the General with a group of staff officers crossed the Channel in a destroyer and made a personal reconnaissance of the Calais and Dunkirk areas to enable him to make recommendations to the War Office upon the next phase of operations. In the meantime, the 1st Canadian Infantry Brigade, with considerable numbers of other troops attached, had been prepared for action and had moved to Dover, where its advanced flight, full of excited expectation, went on board ship and awaited the order to sail. Once again, however, the order did not come. The decision at the War Office, strengthened by information brought back by General McNaughton on 24 May concerning the state of things across the Channel, was that no good purpose could be served by throwing more troops into the cauldron there; and the 1st Brigade, plunged now into deep gloom, made its way back to Aldershot. During the next three days two more proposals were made for the employment of Canadians in the Dunkirk perimeter; but both were negatived by the War Office on further consideration. The 1st Brigade, accordingly, played no part in the actual drama of Dunkirk. They were, nevertheless, to pay a short visit to France that summer.

The Commander of the Canadian Division was now fully convinced that the most useful immediate function of the troops under his command was active preparation "for the task of direct defence of the United Kingdom". With this in view, on 29 May the 1st Canadian Division and the ancillary troops were constituted into a self-contained body known as "Canadian Force"—"a highly mobile, quick acting, hard hitting reserve", ready to move in any direction against an enemy who might now, conceivably, decide to attack England herself.

The next stage was movement to a central area from which Canadian Force could strike fast and hard at invaders who might succeed in crossing the coast. At the end of May, accordingly, the mobile brigade groups in which the Force was organized moved north from Aldershot by night into the area about Northampton; and here they stood in readiness during "Dunkirk Week", while across the Channel the Navy, the exhausted Army and the R.A.F. held off the triumphant enemy and saved the British Expeditionary Force from destruction by an improvised combined operation which will rank as a classic for all time.

By 5 June the last British soldier had been withdrawn from Dunkirk. On that day it became clear that the Germans proposed to finish France before assailing England. They launched a tremendous offensive against the surviving French armies in position on the line of the Somme; and it was only too apparent that France faced collapse and that it was essential to send what could be collected in the way of a new B.E.F. to support her. The only British formations now remaining on continental soil were the 1st Armoured Division and the 51st (Highland) Division (which was largely destroyed at St. Valéry a few days later); but the Government resolved to despatch from England every division fit to move. This, unhappily, meant for the moment only the 52nd (Lowland) Division and the 1st Canadian Division, with the 3rd British Division following somewhat later. Lieutenant-General (now Field-Marshal) Sir Alan Brooke was to command the whole forlorn hope. The Canadians were hurriedly brought south again, and on 8 June they were visited by Their Majesties the King and Queen. By the evening of the next day the advanced elements of the Division were again moving out of Aldershot, this time in the direction of Falmouth and Plymouth. They were bound on as desperate a venture as ever drew men to those ancient ports.

Of the very brief Canadian foray into France which followed, it is enough to say here that the units of the 1st Canadian Infantry Brigade Group, commanded by Brigadier A. A.

Smith, did land in France on the 13th and 14th of June and moved far up country, into the region of Le Mans; that before they came into contact with the enemy the decision was taken in London that, since Paris had fallen and organized resistance by the French armies was virtually at an end, it was hopeless to send more troops across the Channel; and that the troops which had reached France were recalled, while the balance of the Division, which had been preparing to embark, was told that the move was countermanded. By extraordinarily good luck, considering the condition of France at that moment, Brigadier Smith's command actually got back to England with fewer than half-a-dozen men missing; and the whole Canadian field force, bitterly disappointed at the turn events had taken, was re-united in Aldershot. Canadian officers and soldiers, reviewing the recent events, could find in them no satisfaction whatever save that throughout the business they had carried out orders received from higher authority; that they had had to withdraw without meeting the enemy with whom they had hoped to grapple was no fault of theirs.

The British Government's decision to reverse the move to France had found General McNaughton at Plymouth preparing to sail. When the news arrived, he telephoned the War Office and was told by General Dewing that the Canadians were now needed for "another battlefield". What was in the minds of those directing affairs at Whitehall may be gathered from words used by Mr. Churchill on 18 June, four days later:

> What General Weygand called the Battle of France is over. I expect that the battle of Britain is about to begin.

* * * *

The situation of England at this juncture requires, indeed, no laboured exposition. She had saved her army, but the army had left virtually all of its heavy equipment in France; and she was now faced with the imminent threat of invasion by a powerful and ruthless enemy, flushed with victory, who controlled the whole western mainland of Europe. It was a high and terrible moment in her history; but under the inspired leadership of the new Prime Minister, whom the crisis had made, she rose to meet it in a manner worthy of the nation that had conquered Napoleon. During the months that followed her armies dug and sweated on the beaches, the roads and the aerodromes; her navy watched ceaselessly for the invader's barges; her splendid air force—already including many Canadians and superior to the enemy's in all save numbers—shot his attacking squadrons out of the heavens day after day. A new citizen army, the Home Guard, sprang into existence to meet the threat of battalions dropped from the sky; and in the factories, from one end of the country to the other, the workers of Britain bent their backs, seven days a week, to the task of replacing the arms and equipment lost in France and providing those needed for vast new armies. Our business now is to outline the Canadians' share in the events of that amazing summer.

Canadian Force was at once reconstituted, and resumed the role which it had played before the unsuccessful last attempt to save the Third Republic. Now directly under G.H.Q. Home Forces, it again became (in its Commander's phrase) "a hard-hitting mobile force ready to proceed North, South, East or West". The 1st Brigade Group was immobilized for the moment by the loss of its transport vehicles, destroyed in France to prevent them from falling into enemy hands; but during 23-25 June the remainder of the Force rolled out of Aldershot yet once more, bound again for a central area from which a counter-attack might best be launched. The area now selected lay in the immediate vicinity of Oxford, and Divisional

Headquarters was set up on Shotover Hill, which in an earlier and more mannerly war had often seen Prince Rupert galloping out from the city "towards glory and plunder afar".

On 25 June General McNaughton reviewed the situation at a conference of his senior officers. He told them that the Canadians were "a mobile reserve with a 360-degree front"; they might have to operate anywhere in Britain, from the south coast to Scotland, or perhaps in Wales. Theirs was a serious responsibility; for the Canadian Force, along with two British tank battalions and some light armoured units, constituted "the only mobile force immediately available in Great Britain".[1] Although there were many troops in the country, few divisions were yet properly reorganized and the degree of re-equipment which had been possible was "lamentably small". It was not an encouraging picture; but the Canadians, angry and disgusted, on the one hand, at having so far been denied a blow at the enemy, and heartened and upheld, on the other, by the tremendous national revival in progress all around them, were conscious now of having a rendezvous with destiny. Alone, if necessary, or with whatever help their luck might send, they were quite prepared to meet, and do their best to beat, any force of Hitler's that might get past the Royal Navy and the R.A.F.

They kept Dominion Day in Oxford; but their stay there was not prolonged. As the British forces available for immediate action began to increase in numbers and improve in equipment, the plans for the defence of England moved into a

---

[1]Of the British infantry divisions in the country, the most mobile was probably the 3rd, commanded by Major-General B. L. Montgomery. This formation had already received almost complete equipment to replace that lost in France. After the return from Dunkirk, however, only 4,500 men had rejoined it by 6 June; and with reinforcements forming a very high proportion of its strength thereafter, its immediate fighting value was necessarily somewhat impaired. The 52nd Division, which had formed part of the Second B.E.F., had (like the 1st Canadian Infantry Brigade) just returned to England minus most of its transport.

new phase. It was now possible to maintain one mobile corps of two divisions north of the Thames and a second, including the 1st Canadian Division, south of the river. In order to take its place in this new scheme, Canadian Force broke camp on 2 July and moved southeastwards, into the Guildford-Reigate-Westerham area of Surrey and Kent, immediately south of London—the pleasant region of the North Downs. This was to be its normal station for some time to come.

On 7 July the C.-in-C. Home Forces formally asked of the War Office the formation of the new corps, to be known as the 7th Corps, and to be commanded by Major-General McNaughton with the rank of Lieutenant-General. It was to consist of the 1st Canadian and 1st Armoured Divisions, plus the "New Zealand Force" (the major part of the 2nd New Zealand Division, which had lately arrived in England), and selected ancillary troops. The 1st Armoured Division had been evacuated from France, losing most of its equipment in the process. It was now more than willing to fight again, though it was woefully short of weapons, having only 50 infantry tanks and 35 cruisers at the end of June. The Canadian Government agreed to the utilization of General McNaughton's services; and on 18 July, accordingly, he handed over the command of the 1st Canadian Division to Brigadier G. R. Pearkes, V.C., who was promoted Major-General. General McNaughton retained command of Canadian Force as a whole until 21 July, when the 7th Corps officially came into being.

The staff of the new Corps was partly British and partly Canadian. The War Office had provided for it several officers of exceptional brilliance. Notable among them was the Brigadier, General Staff—Brigadier M.C. (later Lieutenant-General Sir Miles) Dempsey, who was later to distinguish himself in the Mediterranean theatre and to command the Second British Army in the invasion of France in 1944. Another was the D.A. & Q.M.G., Brigadier (now Major-General) C. A. P.

Murison, later D.Q.M.G. (A.E.) at the War Office. Canadian born, he had been nominated when an undergraduate by McGill University in August 1914 for a commission in the Royal Artillery, British Regular Army. During 1933-35 he had been G.S.O.2 at the Royal Military College of Canada.

Through that lovely and ominous summer, while the shadow of invasion lay darkly across the smiling southern countryside, the troops of the 7th Corps laboured unremittingly on perfecting their own efficiency against the assault which few doubted would be attempted. Various improvements, based upon experience in France, were made; one of these was the organization of highly mobile reconnaissance units, equipped for the time being largely with motorcycle combinations, and designed for employment on the front, flanks and rear of fast-moving columns of the type in which the Canadians might have to operate in the event of invasion. In exercises special emphasis was laid upon co-operation between infantry and tanks, and upon the training of brigade and battalion groups in rapid movement by road.

The attempted invasion did not materialize; but there is every reason to believe that it was intended. During August, information reached the British authorities of increased assemblages of all types of shipping along the "invasion coast" from Oslo to Brest; concentrations of motor transport were visible; and the Germans were known to be carrying out embarkation and landing exercises on the Channel coast. At the end of the month a 7th Corps Intelligence Summary advised the Corps that all evidence indicated "an advanced stage of land preparedness for an expedition". It added, "An attempt may be made during the first half of September".

During August, moreover, the German air force had begun large-scale attacks upon England which were clearly the prelude to the main operation. These attacks, met by the R.A.F. with an outpouring of skill and courage which is already a

BUCKINGHAM PALACE,
APRIL, 1940

His Majesty The King, with Generals McNaughton and Crerar, watches Canadian troops mount the King's Guard.

BUCKINGHAM PALACE,
APRIL, 1940

The Royal 22e Regiment marches off after mounting the King's Guard.

national legend, led to the greatest air battles ever fought till then in the history of the world. In these battles additional to individuals with the R.A.F., No. 1 (Fighter) Squadron, Royal Canadian Air Force bore its part. The offensive began on 8 August, and was directed in the first instance against shipping and ports. Later in the month inland fighter aerodromes and aircraft factories became its objectives; and finally, on 7 September, on a "gloriously fine Saturday afternoon", the main attack upon London began.

That same day saw the military forces in Britain brought to the final stage of alert. At 8:25 that evening the 1st Canadian Division received the warning code word "Cromwell". Every unit was now to be on four hours' notice to move. Stand-to was ordered at dawn and dusk, and all were warned to be on the alert for parachutists, or enemy agents attempting to land from aircraft or boats.

Each battalion made its final preparations for the anticipated momentous move. An officer of The West Nova Scotia Regiment described the crisis as his unit experienced it:

> The C.O. called a conference for 2200 hrs. to finalize plans for the move which we all expected would come during the next 24 hours. The group for the conference gathered in the Orderly Room Marquee. Planes, enemy planes, roared in a steady procession overhead, as we gathered about the table in the tent dimly lighted by a lantern. Plans were made and orders issued for final preparations for the expected move. A rear party was detailed. Maps were issued, together with sketches of the position of readiness that we would take up if we moved. . . . During the conference a bomb fell, close enough to be heard exploding, thus adding to the realism of this gathering, where we sat about in the dimly lighted tent, in steel helmets and with respirators at the alert. At last we felt sure that our training days were at an end.

On 11 September Mr. Churchill broadcast to the nation, announcing frankly that the enemy's "preparations for invasion on a great scale" were steadily going forward. Pointing out that "if this invasion is going to be tried at all, it does not seem that it can be long delayed", he proceeded:

> Therefore, we must regard the next week or so as a very important period in our history. It ranks with the days when the Spanish Armada was approaching the Channel, and Drake was finishing his game of bowls; or when Nelson stood between us and Napoleon's Grand Army at Boulogne. We have read all about this in the history books; but what is happening now is on a far greater scale and of far more consequence to the life and future of the world and its civilization than those brave old days of the past.

On 13 September it was estimated by Intelligence that shipping sufficient to embark 175,000 men was standing ready in enemy ports opposite the English coast from Harwich to Dungeness. Two days later came the greatest day of the air battle which for weeks past had been raging in the clear skies over the heads of the watching Canadians south of London. On that bright Sunday 185 enemy aircraft were shot down for a loss of 25 British planes.

Had the enemy got the better of the R.A.F., invasion would presumably have become reality, and the 7th Corps would have had the opportunity to put into action the counter-attack measures which it had been practising so assiduously. But the Air Force won its battle; and the enemy did not make the venture. (Nevertheless, the legend of the attempted invasion that failed dies hard; it bids fair, in fact, to be the modern equivalent of the famous last-war story of the Russian divisions who were seen passing through England, one Sunday morning, "with snow on their boots".) By 21 September the Germans' shipping was beginning to move away from the

Channel, and invasion preparations generally were showing signs of decrease. Gradually, the Canadians, who for weeks had been hourly expecting to hear the church-bells that would warn the people of England that Hitler was putting it to the touch, resigned themselves to the fact that their hopes of action had again gone unrealized.

The crisis had been successfully surmounted. The emergency for which the 7th Corps had been created was passing away; and although the men from the Dominion could tell themselves that their presence in Britain and their readiness for action had been an element in making action unnecessary, the fact that after all their alarums and excursions they had yet to meet the enemy was a bitter pill to swallow.

On Christmas Day, 1940, the 7th Corps as such ceased to be; the 2nd Canadian Division, now concentrated in Britain and considered fit for action, came under General McNaughton's command; and, as already noted, a Canadian Corps came into existence.

The New Year found the Canadians in the position which they had taken up during the past summer. The 1st Division was still in Surrey, the 2nd Division, which had moved into Aldershot when the 1st moved out, remained in the barracks there. With spring and better weather in the Channel came the hope that the Germans might yet attempt invasion, and the Corps continued to train hard for the G.H.Q. Reserve role which it had inherited from its predecessor. But England in 1941 did not offer to an invader the relatively tempting prospect which she had presented the year before, and Hitler's intuition had turned in another direction. In May heavy air raids on England came for the moment to an end; in June, Germany attacked Russia. Great Britain, whose coast had been the front line of Freedom's war since the collapse of France, suddenly found herself in the position of an onlooker.

SUSSEX BY THE SEA

Before 1941 was out the Canadian field force moved from Surrey, where the greater part of it had been billeted for more than a year, into the lovely southern county of Sussex, with which the Canadians were to become identified in a still more special manner.

They had had some acquaintance with Sussex even earlier; for in the latter part of 1940 the three brigade groups of the 1st Division had held in succession, each for three weeks, the coastal sector from Worthing to Newhaven. The 3rd Brigade moved thither late in October and was replaced in due course by the 2nd, and it in its turn by the 1st. The 4th and 5th Brigades then did tours of duty in the same area. The task of these brigades while in Sussex was to guard against the possibility of enemy armed reconnaissance raids during the winter months. To their great disappointment, however, such raids did not materialize, then or later; the cautious enemy limited his activity against England to bombing from the air.

The possibility of the Canadian Corps moving from G.H.Q. Reserve into a coastal sector was first discussed in March 1941, when General Brooke, then C.-in-C. Home Forces, suggested such a revision of arrangements to General McNaughton. The latter was prepared to co-operate to the full, but made one proviso: he hoped that their assuming the role of a "static corps" in a coastal sector would not cause the Canadian Forces' claims to form the spearhead of any offensive to be forgotten. General Brooke assured him that there was no danger of those claims being overlooked.

The preliminary to the general move of the Corps was a short sojourn in Sussex by the 2nd Canadian Division, which after being stationed in Aldershot for nearly a year was ready for a change. It was arranged accordingly that the Division would exchange roles for about a month with the 55th Division, then on the coast; the 55th would move to Aldershot and come under the operational command of the Canadian Corps, while the Canadian Division would take over its responsibilities for the defence of East Sussex. The move took place early in July.

The new arrangement committed to Canadian keeping the stretch of coastline from the ancient port of Rye near the Kentish border to west of Newhaven. The Division remained here for more than a month of summer weather, and the Canadian troops made the most of the novel opportunity presented for bathing in the sea. In August they moved back into the Aldershot area, where the majority of them went under canvas.

In the autumn, the Canadian Corps as a whole duly moved into Sussex. The 2nd Division again relieved the 55th in mid-October, and the 1st Division took over from another British Division in the latter part of November. On the 17th of that month Canadian Corps Headquarters moved south from Surrey and relieved the British Corps which had been responsible for the defence of the Sussex coast. At the end of November the 3rd Division, which was now considered ready for an "operational role", likewise moved into Sussex; and the 1st Army Tank Brigade followed just before Christmas. The whole fighting strength of the Canadian Corps, now a very formidable organization, was thus concentrated in Sussex.

It is not for Canadians to attempt to decide between the claims of forty English counties on the score of beauty; but most Englishmen would admit that in any such competition Sussex would at least be entitled to consideration. As for the Canadians who spent so many months there, they will be prepared to say, with Kipling, that their lines were cast

In a fair ground—in a fair ground—
Yea, Sussex by the sea!

From the northern edge of the county the Forest Ridge, heavily wooded, looks across the green fields and pleasant market-towns of the Vale of Sussex to the great rounded Downs on the southern horizon. The South Downs dominate Sussex. They lie close to the sea, running West from Beachy Head towards Winchester. From the beaches they rise in relatively gentle slopes to the summit of the ridge; on the north, however, they present to the traveller driving from London a noble escarpment, far-seen across the country. On paper, their height is insignificant (the highest summits are little more than 800 feet); to the actual beholder, they are a splendid and indeed a majestic sight. Their gentle and solemn beauty provides the background for almost every Sussex landscape, and in the minds of Sussex men they are the symbol of their country, as they are in Hilaire Belloc's verses:

> The great hills of the South Country
>   They stand along the sea:
> And it's there walking in the high woods
>   That I could wish to be. . . .

Some Canadians will remember them, in time to come, with only less emotion.

This southland is historic ground. Scores of generations of Englishmen have stood guard here for their country; and the sight of men from across the Atlantic sharing the watch in this latter-day crisis was something to stir the imagination. When the Canadian Minister of National Defence (Col. the Hon. J. L. Ralston) and the Chief of the General Staff (Lieut.-General K. Stuart) visited the 2nd Division in October, 1941, they found Le Régiment de Maisonneuve established in and around Pevensey Castle, on the site of one of the Roman fortresses of the Saxon Shore, and overlooking the spot where the Norman Conqueror landed in 1066; they found, too, that the unit had incorporated in its defensive system Martello towers built in the days of the Younger Pitt as safeguards against invasion by Napoleon. It was a curious turn of fortune's wheel that brought these French-speaking soldiers from Montreal, many of them certainly descendants of seventeenth-century Norman settlers, to hold such positions against Adolf Hitler. And from Pevensey Levels the Minister's party drove on to Hastings, where they visited The Royal Hamilton Light Infantry; they passed thence to the ancient and picturesque village of Winchelsea, held by troops from Toronto—The Royal Regiment of Canada; and driving on past the ramparts of Camber Castle (built by Henry VIII to defend Sussex against the menaces of his time) they came in the evening to Rye, and found there the pipers of The Essex Scottish, men recruited on the banks of the Detroit, playing beside the waters of the Rother.

Once installed in Sussex, the Canadian Corps found itself responsible for some eighty miles of English coast, from east of Hastings to the Hampshire border, and including the valuable port of Newhaven and the populous borough of Brighton. The keeping of this sector was no small honour and responsibility. From it good routes lead north towards London, and among the coastal areas of England this was one of those most likely to attract the potential invader who lay in strength on the French coast less than 50 miles away. The Canadians, moreover, had to provide not only against full-dress invasion but also against seaborne or airborne raids.

Before the Corps assumed responsibility for the sector much careful thought had been given to the tactical problems involved; and as soon as it took over Corps Headquarters issued instructions providing in detail for every likely emergency. Careful attention was given in particular to the possibility of airborne attack. Thereafter the troops were thoroughly exercised in their new role, and much sweat was expended on the construction and improvement of defences along the coast and round about the Downs. Throughout the period during which the Corps retained responsibility for this front, the modes of defence were constantly under reconsideration and revision. There is every reason to believe that had the enemy obliged by attempting invasion, he would have met with very limited success along the Sussex coast.

The Corps instructions thus drawn and maintained were not entitled "Plans for the Defence of Sussex"; they were called "Plans to Defeat Invasion". The distinction reflected the mood in which the subject was approached; and this mood may in turn have owed something to the higher command under which the Canadians were now operating. On moving into Sussex, the Canadian Corps passed under the operational control of South Eastern Command. About the same time that the Corps moved, General Paget was appointed Commander-in-Chief Home Forces, and was succeeded as G.O.C.-in-C. South Eastern Command by Lieutenant-General B. L. (now Field-Marshal Sir Bernard) Montgomery. During his time in Kent and Sussex General Montgomery left no doubt in the minds of those under his command that his conception of defence was, to say the least, dynamic. He inculcated into his troops the determination to destroy every German soldier who might have the temerity to set foot in England. He demanded of them the highest standard of efficiency and of physical fitness; and the Canadians found that serving under him, even in what are normally known as "static conditions", could be a strenuous business.

* * * *

In moving from the interior to the coast the Canadians nourished hopes extending beyond the English beaches. Even if the enemy would not come to them, they hoped for an early opportunity of going to him. The Canadian field force had been confined to the United Kingdom since the abortive operations in France in 1940, and men were growing tired of inactivity. One detachment, it is true, drawn from the 1st Division, and largely from The Edmonton Regiment and the Royal Canadian Engineers, had had the good luck during the summer of 1941 to participate in a distant enterprise, the expedition to Spitsbergen. Geographically this was a great adventure, carrying a detachment of Canada's army to the very roof of the world. In other respects, however, it was a disappointment, for once more it brought no contact with the enemy; and it concerned only a few hundred men.

Nobody ever doubted that ultimately there would come a great offensive which would give the Canadians their fill of fighting on the continent; but in the meantime they hoped for subsidiary operations which would give them the chance of measuring themselves against the Hun. From the time of the move into Sussex, various schemes for the employment of Canadian troops in raids against the Germans on the coast opposite were considered, and Canadian commanders urged upon the British authorities concerned the desirability of their men being given a full share in any raiding plans, to give them a taste of the action for which they were so eager and some battle experience. No such project reached the stage of action until 22 April, 1942, when about fifty specially-trained men of The Carleton and York Regiment participated in a Commando raid led by Major (later Brigadier) Lord Lovat and directed against the Hardelot area near Boulogne. For the Canadians, unfortunately, this little enterprise was just another fiasco. The naval craft which carried them failed to put them ashore, and while they came under German fire they took no actual part in the operation.

A much larger project was soon in the air. The great combined raid on Dieppe, which after long preparation and several postponements caused by weather conditions was finally carried out on 19 August 1942, is far too big a subject to be dealt with here; it must await the publication of a separate study. Only a brief reference is possible in this place.

Although the outline plan for the raid had been drawn before Canadians became concerned in the enterprise, in its execution it became primarily a Canadian operation. About five-sixths of the whole military force involved came from the Dominion, while the Military Force Commander was the G.O.C. 2nd Canadian Division, Major-General J. H. Roberts. The assaulting force was drawn largely from General Roberts' Division, with the addition of a battalion from the 1st Canadian Army Tank Brigade. Three British Special Service Units (Commandos) were also engaged.

This first battle of the Canadian Army in Europe in this war was by far the largest of the many combined raids that have been directed against the German-held coasts of Europe. It was also the only one in which tanks were employed.

Dieppe was a strong position; those responsible for the operation sought to divert the attention of the German High Command from Russia and they required knowledge of the German installations and methods of defence for application when the invasion of the Fortress of Europe must be undertaken. It was known in advance that the operation was one of exceptional danger; and as it turned out the losses suffered by the Canadian troops were very heavy. It was a considerable time before the 2nd Division, with the ranks of two of its brigades full of reinforcements, attained once more the degree of battle-worthiness which it had reached before the operation.

From the strictly Canadian point of view, it should be said that it was apparent from the time when it was first projected that the Dieppe operation was a task which could be entrusted only to troops of very high quality. It was and is obvious, moreover, to every one who knows the Canadian Army Overseas, that the ordinary Canadian soldier in Britain would have been violently resentful had such an enterprise taken place in 1942 without the participation of the Canadian force there which had waited so long, so eagerly and yet so patiently for action. The Canadians were the obvious people for this dangerous job, and General Montgomery offered it to them accordingly. It must also be said that, in spite of the bad luck and the losses, in the weeks following Dieppe all ranks of the Canadian Army Overseas felt a new confidence and a new pride. The army that had suffered so many disappointments and frustrations had shown that it could fight in the manner of the men of 1914-18; and Lieutenant-Colonel Merritt's Victoria Cross, earned by almost incredible gallantry ("It wasn't human, what he did", said an officer who was with him to the very end) served as a symbol of something more than merely individual valour.

From a larger point of view, more recent happenings upon the coast of Normandy have placed the operation in perspective and provided the most effective commentary upon its value to the United Nations. Speaking in the British House of Commons in September, 1942, Mr. Churchill said: "The raid must be considered a reconnaissance in force. . . We had to get all the information necessary before launching operations on a much larger scale. . . . . . I personally regarded the Dieppe assault, to which I gave my sanction, as an indispensable preliminary to full-scale operations".

In June, 1944, the "full-scale operations" were launched. The perilous enterprise to which the people of the Allied countries had looked forward with so many hopes and fears was carried out, by a force which included a Canadian assault division, with complete success and with smaller losses than even the most sanguine had ventured to anticipate. When in the course of a few days men fully realized that the thing had really happened—that General Eisenhower's Armies had breached the Westwall at a blow and established themselves solidly in France—the name of Dieppe was suddenly on many lips. It was apparent to every informed observer that the experience gained in that costly but essential undertaking had been the foundation of the success of the most momentous operation of war ever attempted.

SURREY, OCTOBER, 1941

Her Majesty The Queen presents new Colours to The Saskatoon Light Infantry.

DIEPPE, 19th AUGUST, 1942

Bombs dropped by a JU 88 bursting among landing craft during the raid.

↓

"SCENE: ENGLAND; AFTERWARDS FRANCE"

Dieppe was itself a symbol of the fact that the war was passing for the Allies from the defensive into the offensive phase. It fitted into the general pattern of Allied strategy, which had been determined, for the moment, on the basis of "holding the enemy on the French shore" (the phrase is Mr. Churchill's), in order to assist the Russians in their gigantic struggle on the Eastern front and distract the Germans' attention from plans for a great enterprise in Africa.

On 8 November 1942 this enterprise began. Powerful British and American forces landed in French North Africa, and in co-operation with the Eighth Army advancing from Egypt proceeded to clear the enemy out of the continent. This process was completed in May, 1943, when a very large German army was penned up in the tip of Tunisia and bludgeoned into abject surrender.

Some hundreds of Canadians from Britain participated in this victorious campaign as individuals attached to the British First Army as part of a general policy to give key personnel battle experience. Many more were soon to be fighting in the same area; for the great Allied offensive was about to be extended across the sea into Europe; and now, at long last, a large section of the Canadian force that had waited so long in England moved to a theatre of operations. In June, 1943, three and a half years after its arrival in Britain, the 1st Canadian Division, now commanded by Major-General G. G. Simonds (who in 1939 had been a major on its staff) left the country secretly. Though very few of its members knew it, it was bound for Sicily. On 10 July the Division participated in the Allied assault, landing on the left flank of the famous Eighth Army, of which it now became a part. Thereafter it played a significant role in the conquest of the island. On 3 September it landed on the toe of Italy—the mainland of Europe; and since that time, under the command of Major-General C. Vokes, it has continued to share the toils and glories of the long fight up the peninsula, and has added Ortona, the Liri Valley and the Gothic Line to the honourable distinctions earned in Sicily.

In the autumn of 1943 the Canadian force in Italy was built up into a Corps. The 5th Canadian Armoured Division disembarked at Naples early in November, whereupon Major-General G. G. Simonds took command, to be succeeded at the end of January by Major-General E. L. M. Burns. Thus on Italian soil, with the further addition of large numbers of Corps Troops, the 1st Canadian Corps was re-created, again under the command of General Crerar. Subsequently the latter, returning to the United Kingdom to take a higher command, handed over to General Burns. In May of 1944 the Corps, in its first action as a Corps, broke through the centre of the Adolf Hitler Line and added a bright new page to Canadian Military History.

The main Canadian field force, however, still remained in Britain; and there, in the meantime, the tempo had quickened perceptibly and purposefully. Men had no doubt now that the grand assault on the Germans in Western Europe could not be very long delayed. The trend of events, indeed, was not hard to interpret. In the spring of 1943 arrangements were made to relieve the Canadians of their local responsibilities in Sussex, that they might train undisturbed for the great task ahead. These arrangements, in effect by the first week of June, 1943, resulted in freer movements of Canadian formations about Britain. Both the Armoured Divisions moved east that summer, spending considerable time in a training area in Norfolk; and the 3rd Division's Brigades, after a period of combined operations training in Scotland, were concentrated by September in the coastal area of Hampshire.

By this time it was coming to be known within the Canadian Army that this 3rd Division—commanded now by Major-General R. F. L. Keller—was training for a very special and perilous task: it had been selected as an assault division, and was developing and practising the technique to be used in breaking the hard shell of Hitler's *Festung Europa* when the day came. Before 1943 was out, the technique—based mainly upon the lessons of Dieppe—had been tested in exercises and found good.

At the same time, Canadian officers who had fought and won in Italy were returning to the United Kingdom to lend the Canadian Army there the benefit of their experience. General Simonds came back to take command of the Canadian Corps remaining in England, with the rank of Lieutenant-General; while many officers who had served under him in the 1st Division came back likewise to take appointments in his new command. And General Crerar, after six months in Italy, returned to become G.O.C.-in-C. First Canadian Army; for General McNaughton, the distinguished chief who had presided over the upbuilding of that Army, was deprived by a turn of fortune's wheel of the opportunity of commanding it on the day for which it had been created.

On 27 December, 1943, Lieutenant-General K. Stuart, formerly C.G.S. at Ottawa, now became Chief of Staff at Canadian Military Headquarters, and acted as Army Commander until March, 1944, when General Crerar arrived from the Mediterranean. The first Canadian senior officer to reach England in 1939 now succeeded to the chief Canadian field command.

By this time, it was a well-advertised fact that the Allies were going to strike soon in Western Europe: only the precise

SUSSEX, 1942. *Canadian tanks manoeuvring.*

(From a watercolour by Capt. W. A. Ogilvie.)

SUSSEX, 1943

A typical farm billet. (From a watercolour by Major C. F. Comfort.)

place and date remained secret. At the New Year of 1944, *The Times* of London had quoted *Henry IV:*

> I will lay odds that, ere this year expire,
> We bear our civil swords and native fire
> As far as France: I heard a bird so sing,
> Whose music, to my thinking, pleased the King.

It was a sound prophecy. Early on the morning of 6 June a storm of steel struck the Germans on the coast of Normandy; and Allied troops poured ashore to begin the stupendous operation that was to liberate Western Europe and put an end to the Third Reich. General Keller's splendid division was in the van of the assault; and the rest of the Canadian force that had waited so long for this moment was not far behind. The English phase in the history of the Canadian Army Overseas was finally at an end.

II

THE WEAPON ON THE ANVIL

THE experience of the Canadian Army Overseas in the present war has been in striking contrast with that of 1914-18. During the last war the British Isles were a base for operations which were continuously in progress in France. The Canadian force which arrived in England in October 1914 went to France in the following February, and from that time on the main Canadian field army was actively engaged there. The Canadian troops in England, while numerous enough, were mainly those engaged in advanced training, on the strength of base establishments, on leave from the front, or recovering from wounds received in action.

In the present war, on the other hand, the greater part of the Canadian field army remained in the United Kingdom until the summer of 1944, without engaging in large-scale operations. But although this was a period in which Canadians were denied the chance of meeting the enemy, it was not a period of inactivity. In the eyes of those commanding the Canadian Army it appeared as an opportunity such as that army had never enjoyed in the last war; an opportunity for perfecting itself by training and exercise before the time came for its actual employment on the field of battle, and for improving its organization and equipment to the point where it could take the field in the highest state of efficiency which care and intelligence could produce. We have already said that the First Canadian Army was by 1944 certainly the best-trained army the Dominion had ever possessed. On the eve of battle, indeed, the Army Commander, in a letter of thanks addressed to the various headquarters and base establishments in England which had played their part in preparing it for action, wrote flatly: "I am convinced that we go into action in a state of fitness for war which has not before been attained by any Army."

Any account of the Canadians' course of training in the United Kingdom must fall naturally into three main phases, determined by the course which the war has followed. The first, a short one, was the period in the winter of 1939-40 during which the 1st Division and the ancillary troops were training with a view to joining the B.E.F. in France. The second, much longer, was that in which the chief immediate object of training was to fit the units for the defence of Britain in the event of a German attempt at invasion. The third was the training for offensive operations abroad, which commenced in earnest when the resources of the United Nations, growing as their war effort became better organized and integrated, began to hold out solid hope that the Allies could go over to the attack at a fairly early date.

At the time when the 1st Canadian Division arrived in England in 1939, it had had in effect only elementary training, and was far from ready for battle. As soon as the Division was established at Aldershot, a syllabus was prepared under which individual basic training would begin at once, to be followed by unit training and in due course training on a formation basis.

Before this program could be completed, it was interrupted by events on the continent. First the Norwegian crisis, and then the campaign in the Low Countries, interfered with it, and the training was, in fact, never completed in the form planned.

THE SHADOW OF INVASION

After the return of the 1st Brigade from France in June, 1940, the all-important task was the defence of England. We have already seen something of the manner in which, during the rest of the summer, the Canadians rehearsed the movements demanded by their role of immediate counter-attack. The 1st Division, when under orders for France, had been provided for the first time with complete equipment in heavy weapons and vehicles, which until then it had possessed on only a "training scale". The units had now to accustom themselves to the handling of this full scale of equipment under field conditions, and particularly under conditions of rapid movement. The operational movements about England which have already been described, to say nothing of the exercises specially designed to that end, gave them before the summer was over a great deal of experience in the fine art of moving mechanized forces on the roads of southern England.

When in the late autumn of 1940 it became clear that the imminent danger of large-scale invasion was over for that year, the Canadians began once more the routine of individual training, a course not particularly popular with the troops, but one which was desirable from the point of view of ensuring that every man thoroughly understood his own business and in particular the handling of his own weapons. This went on during the winter of 1940-41; but before the spring came the newly-constituted Canadian Corps was ready for training on a large scale, including exercises to practise its Divisions in the action that would be required if the approaching "invasion season" produced the enemy attack for which the men were fervently hoping.

The first exercise in which the Canadian Corps operated across country on a Corps scale was that of 11-13 February, known as Exercise "Fox". The 1st Division and a large force of Corps Troops took part. The object was to exercise the troops in the movements most important in connection with the Corps role of G.H.Q. Reserve: road moves to a concentration area, an advance to make contact with the hostile forces, and deployment for the attack. The "general idea" was that the enemy was invading Southern England and delivering one of his main thrusts against the Dover area. The action, accordingly, centered in the region of Kent west of Folkestone.

A major concern of this exercise was the problem of traffic control. Now traffic control may seem a dull subject, and moreover somewhat remote from the popular idea of military operations; but in fact nothing is more essential to the successful action of a modern army, and it would not be difficult to find in the history of the present war instances where opportunities have been lost simply because our forces, impeded by their own masses of vehicles, were unable to get forward to grapple with the enemy at the time and place which circumstances demanded. Properly used, the thousands of vehicles provided for a modern army corps have the effect of giving it mobility surpassing the wildest dreams of soldiers of earlier generations; without scientific control, on the other hand, they serve only to block the roads and destroy that mobility which they are intended to enhance. Formations moving at haphazard, with their many guns and vehicles, inevitably become entangled and dwindle into the status of mere obstacles to advance and tempting targets to the enemy.

The roads of England, more than those of most countries, provide special difficulties for the tactician.

Before the Roman came to Rye, or out to
 Severn strode,
The reeling English drunkard made the rolling
 English road.

The Roman, when he came, did his best to undo the mischief; but he left England a long time before the Canadians arrived, and few straight and few broad highways have been built in the country since his day. The military problem of the English road was one that could be solved only by steady application and hard actual practice on the macadam; and Exercise "Fox" was the first occasion on which the new Canadian Corps, as such, tackled the problem.

The result was a serious and salutary shock to complacency. At certain points during the exercise, most remarkable traffic jams developed; the artillery, in consequence, did not get forward; and the infantry, as a further result, were allowed to "attack" without artillery support. It was a useful if disturbing lesson, which left no doubt in anyone's mind concerning the nature of the shortcomings and the means required for overcoming them.

A few weeks later, the 2nd Division and Corps Troops carried out a parallel exercise, known as "Dog". This took place in the Western instead of the Eastern section of the Corps' prospective field of operations, and the centre of activity was the fine Downland region overlooking Chichester. Serious deficiencies in traffic control again came to light, and the lesson which the Corps Commander drew from it was that "everyone's got to become traffic-minded".

These exercises were upon a relatively restricted scale, although they involved a good many thousands of troops and a good many miles of English countryside. In the month of June, 1941, however, the Corps as a whole participated in larger manoeuvres, mounted by South Eastern Command and known as Exercise "Waterloo". About 100,000 troops took part. In this case the enemy was assumed to have begun a large-scale attack on the British Isles involving a series of landings on the East and South Coasts, one of the major thrusts being directed against Sussex. The forces representing "own troops" in the exercise included a British Corps and a British Armoured Division in addition to the Canadian Corps.

The operations were dominated by the splendid ridge of the Downs, from which the "German" troops, represented by crack British formations including a Brigade of Guards, debouched and advanced rapidly northward. The Canadians, moving to meet them, collided with the invaders in and around the agreeable Sussex town of Horsham. Through a noisy night the tide of battle rolled up and down the streets, and it must have been a relief to the harassed inhabitants when the Guards were umpired out. The exercise ended with the "British" forces putting in an attack against the north face of the Downs on the morning of 16 June. On this day the 1st Canadian Division fought against tanks of the 25th Army Tank Brigade. Three years later, in far-off Italy, the fortune of war brought these two formations together again. Between them, they broke the Adolf Hitler Line; and to-day this British Army Tank Brigade wears the Maple Leaf on its tanks as a momento of good comradeship in victory.

* * * *

There would be no point in describing in detail, or even in outline, all the exercises in which the Canadian Corps participated during this period. One more exercise of 1941 must, however, be mentioned: the Army Manoeuvres at the end of September, which were designated Exercise "Bumper".

In terms of the forces involved, these manoeuvres were the largest which ever took place in Britain. They involved two Army and four Corps Headquarters, twelve Divisions (three of them armoured), two Army Tank Brigades and great numbers of ancillary troops. In all, perhaps 250,000 men took part.

Although these manoeuvres were in one sense the climax of the anti-invasion training program, they also looked forward to offensive operations beyond the Channel, and were designed to test the organization of the British Army to that end. By now, the German Army was deeply engaged in Russia, and it was beginning to be apparent that it was going to have, at best, a difficult campaign there. In these circumstances, the immediate threat to Britain was considerably less serious than it had been, and men's minds were already turning to the possibility of a "second front" in Western Europe.

The exercise was based on the assumption that the enemy had made several separate thrusts against England. All except one had been successfully dealt with; but the "Germans" had made rapid progress inland from landing points in East Anglia. In these circumstances, the forces of Southern Command, under Lieutenant-General the Hon. H. R. L. G. (later Field-Marshal Sir Harold) Alexander, were called upon to move against the invaders marching from the east and destroy them. The Canadian Corps, with the 1st and 2nd Canadian Divisions under command, was placed under General Alexander for this purpose.

During "Bumper" the Canadians covered many miles. In the initial stages they left their normal stations for a concentration area in Sussex. Thence they moved into the Southern portion of the Chiltern Hills, to the West of London. Here they made contact with the enemy; and thereafter their part in the exercise took the form of an advance northeast in a great wheel round the capital, pushing him back through the picturesque close country of the Chilterns. There was "fierce guerrilla fighting", particularly around the Hertfordshire town of Hitchin, which the Royal 22e Régiment captured by marching up an unguarded boundary road and subsequently held against all comers. (The incensed enemy that night ran 25-pounders right up to the perimeter and fired into the town at point-blank range, while the "Vandoos" retaliated by hurling "thunder-flashes" from the housetops.) At the end of the exercise the Canadian Corps Headquarters had been established in St. Albans.

In these great manoeuvres, a certain number of actual casualties took place in addition to a great many simulated ones. It was reported that nineteen men lost their lives in accidents, but General McNaughton was able to report to Ottawa that there were no Canadians among them. The Corps' casualties had amounted to nine men seriously and eighty-two slightly injured. In view of the magnitude and realism of the exercise, the Corps Commander considered that this result reflected a satisfactory state of discipline and training among the troops.

Exercises like this are, from the point of view of the production of efficiency, the next best thing to actual operations. They are the field trials of the military machine, the most effective means of ensuring that it will function smoothly in the face of the enemy; they are also the means of discovering weaknesses in the machine which, if undetected until the formations went into action, might have dire consequences. From the point of view of morale, moreover, they have their own special value. They give the soldier new experiences and a welcome change from the too-familiar surroundings of his normal station; and, provided only that the weather is kind (as it was during "Bumper"), he thoroughly enjoys them.

THE BATTLE DRILL IDEA

By this time the men of the Canadian Corps had been serving for two full years, years of disappointment so far as active operations were concerned; and the problem of maintaining their interest in training which had, it might have seemed, led them nowhere, was an important one. Such exercises as have been described were part of the solution; but other developments of this period also made most useful contributions.

One of these was the introduction of what became known as "battle drill". This was not a Canadian idea, for battle drill, so far as it can be said to have had a single origin, began with experiments by the 47th British Division in 1941; it was, however, taken up by the Canadians with great enthusiasm (the Calgary Highlanders, more than any other single unit, seem to have been the pioneers), and battle drill training, it was found, added tremendously to the interest of the average soldier in his job.

The object of battle drill is to fit the soldier for the actual work of combat. It consists in reducing tactics to its bare essentials, and teaching it to the men of a platoon on the basis of a team drill, with clear explanations regarding the objects to be achieved, the principles involved and the individual task of each member of the team and his responsibility for the success of the operations. The aim is to inculcate in every fighting man the highest battle discipline and team spirit, giving him the knowledge of certain basic "plays" which will guide him in any task which may confront him on the battlefield.

On this basis grew up a whole new system of "battle drill training", involving not merely battle drills themselves as above described, but also a high standard of weapon training, "purposeful physical training", fieldcraft, battle discipline and "battle inoculation". Of special interest, alike to the public (whose idea of battle drill was frequently incomplete and distorted) and to the troops themselves, was the process of "battle inoculation" by which men were accustomed to the experience of being under fire by having live ammunition actually fired over their heads or immediately in front of them. In addition to small-arms fire, artillery, grenades and mines were used. In this way men become to some extent inured to the conditions and especially the noises of battle before ever going into action, and are forcibly impressed with the importance of swift movement and constant alertness. Inevitably, and in spite of all precautions, the use of live ammunition has occasioned a certain number of casualties; but the realistic

THE BATTLE DRILL IDEA

Exploding charges simulate the conditions of battle. (The Canadian Black Watch at assault training, Scotland, 1943.)

training provided has certainly saved a much greater number of lives in actual operations.

The battle drill idea permeated field training from this time onwards, and increased emphasis was laid upon large-scale field exercises involving the use of live ammunition. Training areas were marked out where such exercises could be held without danger to the civil population, considerable numbers of whom had to be evacuated. The Canadians made special use of areas on and about the South Downs. Here, in the summer of 1942, were held a succession of "field firing" exercises in which Canadian infantry delivered attacks across country with the support of large forces of artillery firing actual barrages. On 3 August, for instance, the 3rd Infantry

Brigade participated in a scheme not far from the field where Simon de Montfort won his Battle of Lewes in 1264. The scene that day would have astonished Earl Simon. The brigade was supported by the Churchill tanks of the 14th Canadian Army Tank Battalion (which just a fortnight later were in the van of the Dieppe assault) and by three regiments of field artillery. The gunners, firing their 25-pounders from several miles in rear, laid down heavy concentrations in front of the battalions as they advanced.

Such exercises as this had a vital quality of realism which had been lacking in the training of earlier periods. The whole system stemming from the battle drill idea made a most powerful appeal to the Canadians. The new training was the reverse of static; it was quite different from the elementary movements necessarily practised in the early stages of mobilization; it demanded of the individual the highest standard of physical fitness and exertion, and he usually found it absorbing and exhilarating in the last degree. From the point of view of morale it was a great boon; from the point of view of efficiency for battle it was invaluable.

At the same time, large-scale training in combined operations was in progress, involving co-operation with the Navy and considerable periods at sea. In the early summer of 1942 the Canadian troops earmarked for the Dieppe operation moved to the Isle of Wight and there engaged in an intensive program of training designed to fit them for that great assault. After a period of hardening training, two complete dress rehearsals were carried out. The assault force delivered attacks from the sea upon the section of the coast of Dorset about Bridport, a stretch of coastline very similar to that at Dieppe. Such training as this, directed towards an actual and momentous operation, had, needless to say, even more appeal than the battle schools.

During the following winter, the brigades of the 1st Division spent considerable periods at the combined training centres in Scotland, and the basic training in combined operations then received made this Division the first choice for any assault operation which might be proposed for Canadian troops. In the following summer this training bore fruit, when the Division was selected for participation in the assault on Sicily.

THE PRELUDE TO ATTACK

Enough has been said to suggest that by 1942 the defensive outlook of the forces in Britain was changing rapidly to an offensive one. Although the Canadians had always had faith in the ultimate invasion of Europe, there had been a time when that invasion had seemed very distant, and when it appeared more than likely that their first battle would be fought on English downs or beaches. This was now a thing of the past, and every soldier was looking forward to the moment when the order would come to cross the Channel and drive the Germans out of the lands which they had conquered all too easily in 1940.

The new outlook was suitably symbolized by the great South Eastern Command exercise called "Tiger", which General Montgomery directed in May of 1942. This exercise provided the culmination of the training program of the 1st Canadian Corps during the winter and spring season, and was the largest exercise conducted in England that year. It served, incidentally, more than any other single incident, to symbolize the "hardness" of the training in the Command while General Montgomery held sway there. ("South Eastern Command?", one of his staff officers was once heard to say. "South Eastern *Commando* is more like it.")

For the purposes of the exercise, it was assumed that Sussex and Kent were independent hostile countries, while

SUSSEX, JANUARY, 1942

Men of the Royal Canadian Engineers building a bridge under winter conditions.

* * *

REHEARSAL FOR DIEPPE, 1942

A bombed English village serves as a training area for Canadian Churchill tanks.

SUSSEX, FEBRUARY, 1943

The 1st Canadian Army Tank Brigade with their Churchill tanks aligned for a royal inspection.

* * *

CHANGING TANK ENGINES IN A CANADIAN WORKSHOP

(From a watercolour by Capt. W. A. Ogilvie.)

lying adjacent was a powerful but neutral state, Surrey, whose "threats of intervention" were frequently utilized by the Director to influence the course of the operations. The Sussex army was controlled by Headquarters, Canadian Corps, under General Crerar, while the Kent army was directed by the Headquarters of a British Corps. The greater part of the 2nd Canadian Division, which was just beginning its special training for the Dieppe operation, did not participate in "Tiger"; but the 3rd British Division replaced it in the Canadian Corps. The Kent army was strong in armour; the Sussex army in infantry and in the air.

The exercise began with a movement by the Sussex force into the eastern portion of their own territory, where contact was made with the advancing men of Kent. Thereafter, in accordance with General Crerar's plan to fight a withdrawing battle, taking toll of the enemy armour until he had so reduced it as to permit offensive action, the Sussex forces proceeded to fall back. Before this phase was far advanced, however, the Kent army was ordered to retire into its own territory as a result of the threatening attitude of Surrey.

Sussex now resumed the advance and pursued the retreating army to the "frontier" and far beyond it, into the region of Ashford. At the moment, however, when General Crerar was preparing a great attack to crush the Kentish army standing at bay in this area, there was a diplomatic revolution; the baneful influence of Surrey was suddenly thrown into the balance against Sussex, and the Canadian Corps was ordered to withdraw across the frontier forthwith. This withdrawal was not carried out without losses; for the 3rd Canadian Division was badly mauled by enemy armour during the movement. The exercise ended on 30 May.

This outline will suggest the extent to which this exercise tested the troops' endurance. The Canadians, during its course,

THE LONG TRAIL

"Hey, Chum, when are they going to stage a party for me?"

26 November 1941.

Reproduced by permission of the Proprietors of Punch.

made two long advances and two long withdrawals. The Corps was working on a light scale of transport, such as would be available to the advanced elements of a cross-Channel invading force. No motor transport was used to move the infantry, which throughout marched "on its flat feet" in the old-fashioned way. Rations were the "hard scale" only. The weather was unsettled and frequently rainy, and pervasive mud added to the hardships of the troops. In spite of all this, the Canadians came through smiling. General McNaughton's report to Ottawa on the performance of General Crerar's Corps may be quoted: "This Exercise was specially designed to test capabilities to the limit. It lasted eleven days in all, during which some units marched on foot as much as 250 miles, which is about the life of army boots on English roads. Much of this marching was tactical at forced pace. Transport was cut to minimum and troops lived hard under conditions approximating active service. Hardships and heavy tasks accepted by troops most cheerfully and though now very tired they have come through these strenuous tests with enhanced morale and confidence in themselves. Staff work, road discipline and supply arrangements were on the whole excellent."

In the closing stages of the exercise, some infantry units marched as much as 38 miles in about eighteen hours. When Cease Fire sounded, the troops lay down and rested for two days in the areas where they found themselves; they then returned to their normal areas on the Corps front by march route, happily conscious of a tough job well done. Exercise "Tiger" became something of a legend in the Canadian Army Overseas, and even today, when for the Canadians the real thing has long replaced mimic battles, it is not wholly forgotten.

The complete transition to the offensive phase of training was reflected still more clearly in the great Army Manoeuvres held in March of 1943 under the name of Exercise "Spartan".

These manoeuvres must have involved nearly as many men as "Bumper", although the total number of divisions was only ten (of which four were armoured). In "Spartan", Lieutenant-General McNaughton commanded the larger of two opposing armies, composed of six divisions plus large numbers of ancillary troops. The 1st Canadian Division did not participate, owing to the absence of two of its brigades on combined training in Scotland; but the 2nd and 3rd Canadian Infantry Divisions, and the 5th Canadian Armoured Division, all played their parts. For the first time, moreover, two Canadian Corps Headquarters participated in an exercise. The 1st Corps had under its command the two Canadian infantry divisions, while the newly-organized 2nd Corps had the Guards Armoured Division in addition to the 5th Canadian Armoured Division. Also under General McNaughton's command was a British Corps of two infantry divisions.

This was decidedly an exercise in the offensive. (*The Times* described it as "the greatest offensive exercise ever staged in the military history of these Islands", and the description would appear to be accurate.) The army under General McNaughton's command was assumed to be advancing from a bridgehead already established on the continent by another British army. The Canadian Army Headquarters was in fact carrying out the role already tentatively assigned to it in the intended invasion of Europe, the role which the First Canadian Army actually carried out in the summer of 1944.

The exercise need not be described in detail. From the forward edge of its theoretical bridgehead in three southern counties, General McNaughton's "British" army moved forward to encounter the "enemy", commanded by Lieutenant-General J. A. H. Gammell, who rushed to meet them in a manner which the Afrika Korps in its best days could not have bettered. The battle which followed raged over hundreds of square miles of central England, including in its scope the Chilterns and the outskirts of London on the east and the Cotswolds on the west. The 2nd Canadian Corps, under General Sansom, with most of General McNaughton's armour, was on the left, and made a wide outflanking march through the area about Cirencester and Towcester (encountering *en route* some of those problems of traffic control which had troubled the older Canadian formations at an earlier time). The heaviest actual fighting, however, fell to the infantry under General Crerar in the centre, where the city of Oxford, which the Canadians had visited in different circumstances in 1940, found itself for some time the focus of the battle. When the exercise ended, the British force had advanced deeply into enemy territory, and was in position on a line running north-west from London towards Rugby, ready to go forward for a killing blow.

Two features of the manoeuvres call for special note. One is the work of the Engineers. The enemy, falling back before the advancing British forces, carried out enormous theoretical demolitions, including the destruction of something like 200 bridges across the Thames and other streams. Through successive days and nights, as the advance continued, the sappers toiled at reconstructing them, bridging one river after another, sometimes in the face of enemy air attack. The Engineers have occasionally complained of not being sufficiently employed in exercises. No such complaint was heard during "Spartan". The other striking feature was the employment on both sides of very powerful air forces, organized in composite groups including bombers, fighters, fighter-bombers and reconnaissance aircraft. The work of these forces fundamentally affected the action at almost every point. Co-operation between the army and the R.A.F. was organized on the lines indicated by experience in Africa, and was highly effective.

* * * *

From this time forward the training of the Canadian army became directly merged in the task of preparation for the great Allied offensives then being planned. During the early summer of 1943 the 1st Division was training actively for its role in the Mediterranean, and after final rehearsals it sailed in June. While the newspapers reported its triumphs among the Sicilian mountains, the troops still in the United Kingdom sweated at jobs which were more and more closely related to future operations in northwest Europe, and were therefore more and more congenial.

During September of 1943, an exercise called "Harlequin" took place under the direction of the headquarters of the 21st Army Group. The mere name of this formation was a promise of action. There had never been an Army Group in England before, and everyone in khaki knew that this one had been created to command the Anglo-Canadian troops of an Allied Expeditionary Force—the Second British and the First Canadian Armies—in the invasion of Hitler's Europe. "Harlequin" was the climax of many movements of troops about England, and those participating in it were convinced that these and the exercise itself were part of a great scheme of bluff intended to lead the Germans to believe that we were going to invade in 1943. The exercise was in fact closely related to plans for invasion at a rather later date. Its main object was to test the arrangements for moving a great army rapidly through concentration and assembly areas in England to embarkation points, and putting it on board ship. Such a movement is an almost inconceivably complex task of organization. "The more I have seen of war", writes Lord Wavell, "the more I realize how it all depends on administration and transportation." Exercise "Harlequin" was in this respect the rehearsal for the vast operations of June, 1944.

SPITSBERGEN, 1941

Oil stores go up in smoke before the Canadians re-embark for England.

APRIL, 1941

Canadian infantrymen marching home after a two-day exercise.

↓

Few troops were actually embarked, though large forces (including the 2nd Canadian Infantry Division and the 5th Canadian Armoured Division, both of which had moved some time before into the countryside north of Southampton) were marched to the water's edge in the Portsmouth and Southampton areas. Simultaneously, a British Corps was carrying out similar movements elsewhere. To give the Royal Navy an opportunity of practising the loading of vehicles and testing the length of time troops could remain on board without impairing their fighting efficiency, certain units were actually taken for a sail in the Channel. On the basis of the experience of "Harlequin" the final administrative plans for the enterprise ahead went forward.

While the administrative foundations of the great undertaking were thus being laid, Canadians were also playing an essential role in working out the actual tactics of the assault. The 2nd Canadian Division, we have said, had gained at Dieppe the experience which formed the basis for the plan; the 3rd Canadian Division—selected, it has been noted, as one of the assault divisions for the attack—now played a major part in developing from these lessons the new assault technique.

It was in Exercise "Pirate", conducted by the 3rd Division in October of 1943, that this technique was first comprehensively applied. Like the Dieppe rehearsals, this exercise took place on the coast of Dorset; but the scene this time was Studland Bay, adjacent to Bournemouth. It was very necessary that the people of this thickly-populated area should not realize the significance of what was going on; and it was in fact reported afterwards that, "While most civilians were aware that a large-scale amphibious exercise was taking place, to a casual observer very little interest was shown, and to the public generally it was just another large troop movement." One or two "public house keepers, etc." about Southampton, where part of the force

WAITING THEIR HOUR

On December 17th, 1939, the first contingent of the Canadian Army, now in Britain, landed on our shores.

16 December 1942.

TRAINING FOR INVASION

Troops of the 1st Canadian Division on a final rehearsal immediately before embarking for Sicily, June 1943. (From a drawing by Capt. W. A. Ogilvie.)

ACTION AT LAST

A subaltern of the Seaforth Highlanders of Canada briefs his platoon on the deck of a transport en route to Sicily. (From a pen and watercolour drawing by Capt. W. A. Ogilvie.)

embarked, had however been heard to express the view that "this was the real thing". It was indeed, but not as they meant it.

On the morning of 17 October the assault brigade went ashore at Studland Bay. Navy, Army and Air Force had all contributed to the storm of preparatory fire laid down on the "enemy positions". Destroyers put down a heavy bombardment, and in addition the Navy contributed a new and terrible weapon—rocket fire from special vessels. Furthermore, the Army's own self-propelled artillery fired from tank landing craft during the run-in. The R.A.F. also played its part; although unfavourable weather at the airfields prevented it from laying smoke-screens or bombing as required by the plan, cannon attacks were carried out on time. The conclusion afterwards was that the combined fire plan of the three services had "proved itself to be workable and feasible, subject of course to further training based on the detailed lessons learned". The basis had been found for providing for assaulting troops the heavy and immediate support which had not been available at Dieppe, and it is not too much to say that the favourable result of this exercise in October 1943 was the foundation of the successful attack on the coast of Normandy eight months later.

* * * *

When the Canadian army finally went into action, in Sicily in 1943 and in Normandy in 1944, it was, we have said, an extraordinarily well-trained army. Everything had been provided to make it battleworthy—everything short of the experience of battle itself and even in this respect battle knowledge acquired by individual Canadian officers and n.c.o.'s attached to General Anderson's hard-fighting First Army in North Africa had been brought back, disseminated and absorbed. After the Sicilian campaign the same system was followed, when experienced personnel were transferred from the two Canadian Divisions in Italy to the three in England. Now there is no doubt whatever that there is no school like the battlefield for training troops for war; no instructional program, however practical and realistic, can be a substitute for the experience of action. Nevertheless, a really well trained formation will do infinitely better in its first operations than one less thoroughly trained; it will do more damage to the enemy, and it will suffer far fewer casualties itself. In spite of the Canadians' lack of battle experience in fighting formations, they behaved like veterans even in their first fights.

The 1st Division went into Sicily with the Eighth Army, the finest and the most experienced troops in the British service. From them the Canadian Division certainly learned much, and no doubt it taught itself many things on the battlefield which it

CITY OF LONDON, JULY, 1941

The 48th Highlanders of Canada "fight" the London Home Guard amid ruins caused by German air raids.

had not gleaned from the battle schools. Nevertheless, competent observers remarked that in some ways it was actually better fitted for the fighting in Sicily than the British Divisions alongside which it fought. These war-hardened formations had gained their experience in the desert, and Sicilian terrain—"broken country, thick with cover for lurking enemies"—was very different. The Canadians had been taught their trade in England and Scotland, lands much more like that where they were now engaged; and they had been taught it thoroughly. The campaign into which they were now suddenly plunged was rendered the more arduous for them by extreme heat, to which they were quite unaccustomed, and by the fact that they had long been cooped up in transports. In spite of these disadvantages they gave a very good account of themselves.

A similar tale can be told of Normandy. The 3rd Canadian Division had never been in action before 6 June 1944. But they had had the benefit of prolonged and intensive training, and as we have just seen they had played a leading part in developing the technique of the operation in which they were to participate and understood it in every detail. The result was that this "untried" Division went into the assault north of Caen not merely with confidence and determination, but with no small dexterity and skill; and the results which they obtained speak loudly for themselves. The same can be said of the other divisions that followed the 3rd into action. The Canadians had waited a long time; but that time had been turned to remarkably good advantage.

ON THE FRONT LINE

Canadians preparing defence posts on the South Coast of England.

❊ ❊ ❊

CHRISTMAS, 1940

Mr. Massey, High Commissioner for Canada, bringing in the pudding at the Beaver Club, London.

III

THE DAYS OF THE BLITZ

THE years 1940 and 1941 will be remembered in history as the years in which the German Air Force spent its strength in vain against the Fortress of Britain. For three months in 1940 Goering hurled his bombers at the island in a futile attempt to destroy British shipping, cripple the R.A.F. and clear the way for invasion. Baulked by the gallant "few," he then turned with fire and high-explosive upon the cities and towns of England seeking to break the morale of the civilian population. But the spirit of the British people was too strong for him; and in the spring of 1941 the Luftwaffe owned defeat and turned elsewhere.

Men of the Canadian Army witnessed these dramatic events and shared the experiences of the men and women of Britain in those tragic and heroic months. They played no exceptional part; but along with millions of nameless Britons they did their bit and their best. It was a time which Canadians who lived through it will not forget; and from it they drew an inspiration and a pride of association with the British people which has remained for them one of the outstanding features of the war.

* * * *

During the opening months of hostilities there was no enemy air activity against the British Isles. Not until 9 May, 1940, did German bombs fall upon the mainland of Britain. Broadly speaking, the German Air Force was intended to act tactically in close collaboration with the Army. Thus it was only after the conclusion of the campaign which led to the fall of France in June 1940 that the Luftwaffe turned to large-scale bombing attacks upon England.

The months of June and July were spent in preparation for the assault which, the Germans were sure, would culminate in the first successful invasion of Great Britain since the days of William the Conqueror. Such activity as did take place was confined largely to minelaying and reconnaissance flights across the Channel. Finally, on 8 August, as we have seen, the Battle of Britain began. By the end of October it was over. The knock-out blow had failed. The R.A.F. had won one of the decisive battles of modern times; and the people of London had beaten Goering's first great offensive against the capital.

Canadians' direct share in the Battle of Britain was not confined to the gallant few flying in the R.A.F. Fifteen years before the war, Canadian scientists had discovered and developed the practical use of the cathode ray and had gone far in the production of radar equipment. With the aid of these direction finding instruments the energies of the R.A.F. squadrons could be conserved, for they could remain on the ground until required to make a specific attack on an enemy force known to be coming, and were thus spared the wasted effort of constant patrolling.

During the months that followed the Germans relied almost exclusively upon night bombing. The long winter nights lent themselves to this type of warfare, particularly as these raids did not appear to be connected with any large strategic plan save that of crippling production and wearing down resistance. It was a war of attrition—attrition both material and moral. For five months scarcely a night passed without attacks being made upon one or more British cities. Large-scale assaults upon provincial centres began with the famous and savage raid on

Coventry on the night of 14 November. Thereafter the German bombers ranged the country, attacking particularly ports and industrial towns. They spread destruction from Portsmouth and Southampton to Clydeside and Belfast; and at irregular intervals they returned to the capital, in greater or lesser strength, to add to the sum of damage there.

This situation continued, with some variation, through the spring of 1941. But the great raid on London on the night of 10-11 May marked the end of a definite phase in the ordeal of Britain, the first great Blitz. Whereas, 5,520 civilians had been killed in the single month of May, the total for June fell to 406. The raids never wholly ceased, but for a long period after that unpleasant May they were relatively insignificant. In December, 1941, only 34 civilians were reported killed.

The R.A.F. had long been hitting back at Germany. By 1942 it was strong enough to strike effectively. It was in retaliation for its blows that the enemy, in April, launched one of his most cowardly assaults—the series of attacks on cathedral towns known as the "Baedeker" raids. In spite of these, the number of civilians killed that month was less than 1,000. Such comparatively concentrated raids on inland targets were very exceptional; the enemy greatly preferred "hit-and-run" attacks on coastal towns. Such operations, the most inexpensive form of air activity against England which he had yet devised, were frequently carried out in daylight by aircraft, flying singly or in small groups, dashing in from the sea, dropping their bombs and retiring hastily seaward again.

Although the enemy's "scale of effort" against Britain ebbed and flowed somewhat, it remained comparatively small until 1944. He had long been breathing threats of retaliation against Britain, however, for the devastation wrought in Germany by the British and latterly the United States Air Forces. In February he mustered considerable forces for attacks on

London which were the heaviest since 1941, but were nevertheless insignificant compared with those which the capital had then withstood. The month's toll of civilian dead was 961.

These raids were the prelude to another form of German retaliation, more vicious and more indiscriminate: the pilotless aircraft or flying bomb. On the night of 12-13 June (nearly a week after the Allied landing on the coast of Normandy) a few robots were sent over England by way of trial; serious attacks began three nights later, and during the months that followed, while the tremendous drama of the new Battle of France unrolled itself on the continent, the people of London and Southern England underwent a second great ordeal, less terrible than the first in terms of loss of life, but in some respects perhaps a harder test of nerve. The "doodlebugs", as the R.A.F. pilots who destroyed so many promptly christened them, might come at any hour of the day or night; and their great blast effect made them extremely damaging to buildings. A particularly high proportion of the casualties were caused by flying glass. By 2 August, 4,735 people had been killed by the new weapon. But the British, who had faced Goering's multitude of bombers without a tremor when things were at their worst, were hardly likely to give in to these nasty mechanical contrivances at a time when Allied armies were already pushing the Germans back across Western Europe into rout and ruin.

Such has been the general shape of the German air attacks upon England. Let us turn to the story of the Canadians' share in these events.

A GRAND-STAND VIEW

While the great aerial drama of the Battle of Britain was being played out in the summer of 1940 the Canadian troops found themselves occupying the front stalls. From their camps in Surrey they saw the mass formations of German bombers

BATTLE OF BRITAIN

Canadian soldiers in Surrey watch German bombers on the way to London, September, 1940.
(From a watercolour by Colonel Louis Keene.)

flying overhead; they watched the fighter planes of the R.A.F. climbing to meet them; they witnessed many of the "dog fights" so reminiscent of the last war. Sometimes they heard the rattle of machine-gun fire above them; and day after day they gazed up at the thin white vapour-trails of the planes flying three, four and five miles above the surface of the earth.

Often these battles in the sky seemed remote and detached, something belonging to another sphere; on other occasions their grim reality was brought home by the sight of planes streaming fire and smoke as they plunged towards the earth followed at times by lazy white blobs of silk. Sometimes the onlookers themselves suffered casualties.

It was during one of the earliest daylight raids that the Canadian Army Overseas suffered its first loss of life as a direct result of enemy action. On 6 July high-explosive bombs were dropped in Aldershot, killing three soldiers and wounding one officer and 28 other ranks of the Royal Canadian Ordnance Corps. These men's unit was employed at the time in servicing motorcycle combinations for the Reconnaissance Squadrons. Despite the attack the work was completed and the machines delivered on schedule. That Ordnance—once regarded as very much a rearward service—should be the corps to suffer these first casualties was a symbol of the changes that had come across the face of war.

On 15 August the West Nova Scotia Regiment captured their first enemy prisoner. The unit's War Diary tells the story:

> The Company Commander's conference was badly disorganized when an aerial dog-fight started overhead. Actually Orders called for a cessation of all movements around the O.P. area, but everyone forgot Orders in their excitement over the dog-fight. A flight of nine British fighters had intercepted a flight of twelve German bombers. This was something new to most of those present, who were

viewing *real* war and hearing the rattle of M.Gs. fired in earnest for the first time. Doubtless there were few who realized or thought of the grimness of the "show" which they were thoroughly enjoying. The British A.A. fire broke up the German formation and gave the fighter planes their opportunity, which they apparently made good use of to the excitement and enjoyment of the group of officers and men gathered to receive Orders for tomorrow's *mock* war. In very short order five or six of the German bombers were knocked off by the R.A.F. and one bomber, trailing smoke from its tail, passed over our O.P. Two of the crew bailed out. One parachute did not function, the other did and drifted with its occupant in the direction of the O.P. When it was seen that the German was going to land near us there was much loading of rifles and fixing of bayonets and drawing of revolvers, accompanied by threats of what would befall this enemy when he landed. Finally he did drop down a short distance from the O.P. and landed in a group of men large enough to have captured a whole battalion. Despite the threats that had been made our men did not "polish off" the German. Quite the contrary, within a few minutes they had his wounds, of which he had several, bandaged with their field dressings and some were offering him smokes. The parachute disappeared in remarkably short order having been cut into small pieces for souvenirs. The *Prisoner* was hustled into our ambulance and his wounds were properly dressed after which he was taken under guard to Div. H.Q. where he was handed over to the Div. I.O. and a receipt obtained for him. This is our first prisoner and is in fact the first prisoner taken by the 1st Canadian Division.

Three days later men of the Edmonton Regiment saw a squadron of enemy planes, flying over their camp at a great height, engaged by Spitfires and Hurricanes. Three aircraft were seen to fall and officers and men rushed to find them. One man came back with a German pilot's helmet and identity discs and others with pieces of the plane. The propensity of soldiers to collect souvenirs upon such occasions was strongly discouraged officially; but it was difficult to check, and many bits of wreckage found their way into Canadian kit bags.

During August Canadian units suffered further casualties. On the afternoon of 16 August the Holding Units at Bordon, near Aldershot, were attacked by six enemy bombers. Three men, including one officer of the Carleton and York Regiment, were killed, and eleven wounded. Two days later four Messerschmitt 110's, flying only 50 feet above the ground with all guns firing, attacked a Royal Canadian Army Service Corps unit in Surrey. A corporal was killed while directing men into slit trenches, and two privates were wounded. On 25 August bombs were dropped in the camp area occupied by the Royal Canadian Regiment. One man was killed and four injured.

The September records are full of accounts of enemy attacks, of dog-fights witnessed and of the dull red horizon in the direction of London which gave indication of the great raids upon the capital. Scarcely a day passed without the units hearing the ominous drone of German bomber formations attempting to get through to London. Let one quotation from a unit diary set the atmosphere of the time:

> Heavy air raids again tonight. The sound of bombers was heard occasionally and the A.A. fire over London was very heavy. The shells could be seen bursting like stars all across the horizon. At the same time great fingers of light from the search-light batteries were constantly moving across the sky. The whole thing gave the impression of a 1st of July fireworks display; but being so far away from it we have, as yet, failed to understand the grimness of it.

Although the troops fought back with their machine-guns when the enemy was low enough, more often they were required to take cover when the sirens sounded. And with the increase in the number and intensity of the raids this meant long and frequent sojourns in slit trenches. On 15 September, the great day of the Battle of Britain, there were no less than four alarms varying in length from twenty minutes to seven-and-a-half hours. Long periods spent in the cramped quarters of a narrow and sometimes muddy trench were not regarded with any great favour by the troops, who grumbled about it as soldiers have grumbled for centuries. When high explosive bombs began to drop in the near vicinity, however, there were few men who were not quick to appreciate the advantages of cover. The diarist of an infantry unit wrote of one occasion:

> Bombs could be heard clearly screaming down, and the nightly coterie of sky-gazers around Battalion H.Q. did some hasty ducking for cover. The sand bagged A.A. pit across the road was filled to overflowing with men piled in any old way one on top of the other. The A.A. gunners were heard to remark that they 'guessed they'd have lots of help enlarging the pit tomorrow'.

It was during the September raids that two officers, Lieut. (later Captain) J. M. S. Patton and Captain (later Major) D. W. Cunnington, both of the Royal Canadian Engineers, won respectively the first George Cross and George Medal awarded to any members of the Canadian Army.

On the morning of 21 September an aircraft factory in Surrey was attacked by enemy planes. One of the bombs, a 500-pounder, penetrated the factory roof, passed through a wall at the end and came to rest on the concrete outside one of the buildings without exploding. As its explosion where it lay would cause serious damage it was urgently necessary to render it harmless. A company of Canadian Engineers who had been employed on repair work in the neighbourhood were asked whether they could provide a bomb disposal squad. The company had no such squad, but Lieut. Patton, who had reported to the unit less than four days before as a reinforcement officer, immediately went to the spot. Having had no training in bomb disposal he could not "disarm" the bomb; he therefore resolved to remove it bodily, and proceeded to send for a truck and a length of cable. At this point he was joined by Captain Cunnington, and the two officers, with the assistance of British Home Guards, coolly rolled the bomb on to a piece of corrugated iron which was then attached to the truck with the cable. With one of the Canadians driving, the bomb was towed to an old crater at a safe distance, where it duly exploded, quite harmlessly, some hours later.

"A DREADFUL AND IMPASSIONED DRAMA"

The first great air attack upon London, we have said, was launched on Saturday, 7 September, 1940. That afternoon about 375 enemy bombers and fighters, following the line of the Thames and fighting all the way, penetrated the south-eastern portion of the city. For several hours bombs screamed down, damaging docks, gasworks and tenement houses. Great fires—timber fires, pepper fires, rum fires, rubber fires, sugar fires, and tea fires—spread for miles along the river's edge, covering the whole London area with a pall of pungent smoke. As a Canadian senior officer said, the scene in the city that day provided an all-too-vivid illustration of Jomini's famous definition of war: "a dreadful and impassioned drama".

Such was the beginning of London's ordeal, which went on thereafter for many months. The attacks took their toll of Canadian soldiers stationed there, as well as of those visiting the city when on leave. The administrative headquarters of the Canadian Army Overseas was situated in the heart of central

"RIVER GUNSITE"

Canadian gunners on the Thames Estuary, 1941.
(From a gouache drawing by Capt. W. A. Ogilvie.)

"CHANNEL WATCHERS"

Canadian Bofors gunners on the Sussex Coast, 1943.
(From a watercolour by Major C. F. Comfort.)

London, hard by Trafalgar Square where Lord Nelson, high upon his column, looks down the broad stretch of Whitehall past the old Banqueting Hall of James I to the Houses of Parliament. For a time this Headquarters was literally in the front line, more directly exposed to enemy attack than any other part of the Canadian Army. (This was a situation which struck veterans of the last war as a strange and perhaps not wholly unwelcome reversal of the course of nature.) In that autumn of 1940 many bombs fell close, and while the building housing Canadian Military Headquarters was not actually struck the work of the Headquarters suffered serious handicaps.

All civilian employees were, at that time, required by British regulations to take shelter in the sub-basement on the sounding of the air raid warning. Military members of the staff continued to work until watchers on the roof gave warning that enemy aircraft were overhead or until the sound of nearby bombing could be heard; then they, too, were ordered to take cover. The loss of working time thus incurred in the days of daylight raiding was considerable. In an effort to cope with the work, typewriters were carried to and from the shelters. Eventually it became the custom for everyone to remain at his or her desk until the local building alarm indicated imminent danger. The decline of daylight raiding ended the nuisance; and the staff was not sent to the shelters once between the end of 1940 and 20 January 1943, when a hit-and-run noonday raid led to the alarm being sounded.

The first casualty among the staff of Canadian Military Headquarters occurred on 24 September 1940 when a Sergeant of the Corps of Military Staff Clerks was injured at the London Central Y.M.C.A. where he lived. The first officer casualty occurred three days later. Although there were many near misses, there was no serious damage at C.M.H.Q. until the night of 10-11 October, when there was a miss so very near as to be

A BOMB AT THE BACK DOOR

The results of a (very) near miss at Canadian Military Headquarters, London, 11th October, 1940.

virtually a hit. Shortly after midnight a heavy bomb landed in Pall Mall East, close to the building's back door. The force of the explosion blew in windows and glass partitions, and splinters scarred the north face of the building. A water main was broken, flooding the sub-basement; the women clerks and stenographers who, during the heavy raids, were allowed to sleep in the shelters, were driven out by the rising water. Flying glass caused seven casualties (luckily, none serious) among military personnel in various parts of the building. The damage put both the elevators and the heating system out of action for some time, a state of affairs which obtained in many a London building in those days.

In the months which followed the almost continuous attacks from September to November, London had something of a respite, and there was a noticeable revival in the life of the West End. There were occasional heavy enemy blows (the great fire raid on the City proper on the night of 29-30 December was a very notable example), but these were exceptional. The spring of 1941, however, while it brought no recurrence of steady raiding, did bring the heaviest single attacks the capital had suffered. The first of the new series of raids came on the night of 8-9 March. A particularly bad incident took place at the Café de Paris in Coventry Street, near Leicester Square, where a bomb fell in the midst of a throng of merrymakers, killing and injuring many. Four of the dead were Canadians, two of them non-commissioned officers of C.M.H.Q., which thus suffered its first fatal casualties.

Of all the raids on London, the most unlucky for the Canadian Army was that of the night of 16-17 April, the most savage the city had yet suffered. It was an all-night attack, delivered in clear starlight (for the moon rose late) by perhaps 450 bombers. For hours the sounds of aircraft-engines and gunfire and the scream of bombs were continuous. When daylight neared and the Germans, like evil spirits at cockcrow, made haste home, London bore many new scars; and the Canadian army had suffered the heaviest casualties it had yet sustained by enemy action in any single incident. Twenty-two Canadian soldiers were killed, ten of them in the Victoria League Club on Malet Street, a popular hostel which was totally destroyed. The Royal Canadian Artillery lost eleven men in two incidents in southern suburbs; in one of these, seven men were killed when a bomb struck a vehicle in which they were riding. C.M.H.Q. had five fatal casualties. Both the Royal Canadian Navy and the R.C.A.F. also had men killed.

At the height of the raid, an Auxiliary Fire Service pump was on its way through the littered streets of Beckenham in south-eastern London to one of the innumerable fires, when a bomb fell close to it, injuring its crew. The pump's petrol tank was pierced by a splinter, and almost instantly the vehicle was enveloped in flames. Gunner Jack Chambers of the Royal Canadian Horse Artillery was nearby. With complete disregard for his own danger he rushed forward through the blazing curtain and helped to pull one of the firemen to safety. He then turned back into the furnace and made a gallant effort to rescue a second man; but this was frustrated by the raging fire. Gunner Chambers' courage was rewarded with the George Medal.

The raid of the night of 10-11 May, as already said, was the last heavy attack suffered by London in this period of the war. In it four Canadian soldiers were killed. Materially, it was perhaps the most destructive of all. The House of Commons, Westminster Hall and the Abbey all suffered. A bomb actually struck the great clock of the Houses of Parliament, but did not stop it. There could be no fitter symbol of the spirit of the imperial city than the chimes of Big Ben on that May morning, ringing out from the battered belfry to tell the Empire and the world that the enemy had come and gone.

A BIG WEEK IN LIVERPOOL

After London's, the heaviest raids made upon any British community were those suffered by Liverpool and the other towns along the Mersey River. The first attacks fell here in November and December 1940. There were two serious raids in March of 1941, another in April; and then in May came seven successive nights of bombing, "a form of continuous attack inflicted on no other provincial target".

It so happened that one unit of Canadian troops shared the ordeal of Merseyside at this time. They helped to fight the flames and succor the injured; and when all was over they won praise for the work that they had done. Many Canadian units exerted themselves similarly at other places; but the circumstances at Liverpool were special, and as we cannot tell the story of every unit, the story of this one must stand as a type.

In March 1941 the decision was taken to transfer the Canadian Transit Depot (which was staffed by the Lorne Scots) to Liverpool so that it might be near the principal embarkation and disembarkation ports then used by the Canadians. The buildings taken over for the purpose were known as the Seaforth Barracks. They were situated about four miles from the centre of the city and a few hundred yards from the waterfront. The whole camp covered the area of a large city block and consisted of permanent brick buildings and Nissen huts. On 12 March the main body of No. 1 Canadian Base Depot arrived at Liverpool. They were just settling in their new quarters that evening when the wail of the siren announced the beginning of a raid.

The attacks on this and the following night were heavy though not especially concentrated. There were many hundreds killed, widespread fires and much damage to property. The moonlight reflected upon the waters of the Mersey guided the raiding aircraft to their destinations and bombs were dropped on the waterfront near the barracks occupied by the Canadians. A "land mine" fell in the neighbourhood, knocking a row of civilian dwellings over like so many houses of cards. Windows were broken in the barracks.

Following this noisy reception the Canadians spent a month of comparative quiet. The barracks were put into a more habitable condition, the broken glass being replaced by tar paper. The men were given special instruction in dealing with incendiary bombs; and before long they were given an opportunity to apply the knowledge thus acquired in a very practical way. On the night of 16 April another attack was delivered against the city, lasting from half-past ten at night until four o'clock the following morning. Several districts were showered with incendiaries and many fires were seen. Incendiaries landed on several of the barrack buildings but were all quickly extinguished before any harm was done. On the 24th and 25th there were more alerts but no real attack and the remainder of the month passed quietly. It was the calm before the great storm of May, the week during which more than 2,000 bombs were dropped and 1,500 people were killed.

The attacks began on the first day of the month. The Canadians at the Seaforth Barracks were not seriously involved in the first raid, but on 2 May a parachute mine fell about one hundred yards away. Several nearby houses were demolished and a number of people killed and injured. The barracks suffered considerably from blast. Windows were again ripped out, and one wall of the Sergeants' Mess caved in. The roof of one barrack block was also damaged. Many of the soldiers at the depot were men of low medical category awaiting return to Canada, but all of them worked heroically throughout the night. The following day was spent cleaning up the debris of the raid: each day that week, indeed, broken windows were patched up, only to be blown out again by the next attack.

On Saturday night, 3 May, the German bombers came again in force. Thousands of incendiaries were dropped. A number of them fell near the camp but fizzled out in the damp sands of the waterfront. Within Liverpool itself, however, fires were raging through the docks and warehouses. A Canadian officer who witnessed the scene has described it:

> It was an awe-inspiring sight, making even the 'Inferno' of Dante seem a pale and colourless thing. The sky was full of bursting ack-ack shells. Flares dropped by the enemy planes were floating slowly towards the earth, lighting up everything in the vicinity. Bright red tracer

bullets were streaking across the sky, aimed at the flares in an attempt to extinguish them. Along the docks and towards the centre of the city dozens of fires could be seen; in fact it seemed that the whole city was ablaze. Ears were almost deafened by many weird and rather terrifying noises; the continuous drone of planes overhead, the screeching of bombs on their way to the targets, the explosions of the bombs as they landed, the angry roar of gunfire from many guns, and the hoarse shouts of the workers as they tried to communicate one with the other. The acrid smell of explosive, the pungent aroma of burning wood, the thick clouds of smoke and the scarlet glow from buildings etched in the memory of every Canadian a picture that can never be forgotten.

It was on this particular night that Capt. (later Major) D. C. Heggie, R.C.A.M.C., the Depot's Medical Officer, won the George Medal for "conspicuous gallantry in carrying out hazardous work in a very brave manner". The restrained language of the official citation (beginning with the words, "On the night of the 3rd/4th May, 1941, a bomb was dropped near an Army Barracks") does, perhaps, less than full justice to the officer who spent the night under fire amid bombs and falling masonry, binding up wounds and relieving suffering. He forced his way into demolished buildings, directed rescue operations and at times crawled into cellars to administer hypodermics to trapped and wounded civilians. On one occasion he was lowered head-first into the basement of a wrecked dwelling to give morphine to a badly-crushed civilian pinned in the ruins. So it went for eight hours.

Sunday night arrived, and with it the bright moonlight, the wail of the sirens, and the bombs. It was a repetition of the night before, although the bombardment was not quite so intense. But it meant another sleepless night for the citizens

LIVERPOOL, MAY, 1941

Captain D. C. Heggie, R.C.A.M.C., is lowered head-first into a ruined house to assist a wounded civilian. This was an incident of the night's work which won Captain Heggie the George Medal. (From a water-colour by Colonel Louis Keene.)

of Liverpool and the Canadian troops at the Seaforth Barracks. Great damage was done and many more fires were started, but nothing landed in the barrack area. At the usual time on Monday the whole thing began again.

Everyone was beginning to feel the strain of the continuous bombing. Civilians were suffering from lack of food and shelter, and the evacuation of women and children to safer areas was undertaken. They could be seen leaving the city in trucks, carrying a few belongings. The barracks were beginning to look considerably the worse for wear. Hardly a window remained, and the walls of the three-storied block were so badly cracked that it was feared that should another bomb land nearby they would collapse.

Tuesday night brought another raid, and Wednesday still another. The sky was full of bombs coming down and anti-aircraft shells going up; and gradually the attack developed into the most severe yet experienced. Tremendous damage was inflicted and there were many casualties. More incendiaries were dropped upon the camp but were promptly extinguished. In the early hours of the 7th a land mine dropped near the barracks close to the First Aid Post. A dull heavy thud, a split second of silence, and then screams, dust and smoke and falling debris. Capt. Heggie at the First Aid Post was injured in the head. Although bleeding profusely he dragged himself over to the injured Nursing Sisters and managed to pull them clear of the wreckage. He helped to bandage their wounds; then loss of blood forced him to give in. The following day he was evacuated to a Canadian military hospital.

All night long Canadian soldiers laboured on rescue work. They helped the civil defence workers to remove dead and injured from ruined houses; they succoured wounded civilians and helped to extinguish fires; they drove trucks with supplies and acted as guards and traffic guides. Many brave deeds were performed which must go unnoticed here. But that night those who wore the badge of "Canada" upon their battle dress distinguished themselves in the eyes of the citizens of Liverpool.

The black week was over now; and in due course letters of commendation came to the Lorne Scots. The Town Clerk of Liverpool wrote: "I have been directed by the Civil Defence Committee to convey to you their sincere appreciation of the excellent services rendered by detachments of your regiment during and following the recent air raids. The assistance of the troops has been invaluable . . . ."

HIT-AND-RUN

At the beginning of the war the Canadian troops were ill-prepared to fight back against the German raiders. The infantry divisional organization of the day did not provide for anti-aircraft batteries, and when the men of the 1st Canadian Division came overseas the only weapon which they possessed for action against low-flying planes was the familiar Lewis gun of the last war. Early in 1940 General McNaughton proposed to remedy this deficiency by converting one of the machine-gun battalions into a light anti-aircraft regiment, but the suggestion was not proceeded with for the simple reason that there were no Bofors guns to be had. There were, as a result, no units of Canadian anti-aircraft artillery to share in the defence of Britain in the days of the great blitz. But although Bofors guns were lacking, full use was made of the Vickers and Bren guns available. Extemporized mountings, seats and sights were made in Canadian Army workshops and these, fitted to Canadian military vehicles, provided an improvised anti-aircraft defence.

The first Canadian soldiers actually to serve in an anti-aircraft role performed their service at sea. They were Lewis gunners, selected from the infantry and machine-gun battalions of the 1st Division, who in March 1940 were lent to the

Admiralty to protect trawlers plying the waters of the North Sea. Few opportunities of action came to these men, however, and only one team is known to have scored a hit on a German plane.

During the Battle of Britain at least two Canadian units claimed successes against enemy aircraft with small arms fire. On 18 August 1940 two sappers of No. 1 Tunnelling Company with a Lewis gun engaged a German plane near Canterbury and saw it crash; and on 26 November the Toronto Scottish shot a Dornier 17 into the sea near Portslade, Sussex.

In the autumn of 1940 the 1st Canadian Light Anti-Aircraft Battery arrived in England. Several more batteries were subsequently formed overseas during the winter months; and these units were concentrated for training at Colchester in the spring of 1941. As the batteries attained the necessary standard of efficiency they were deployed on operational duties under the Air Defence of Great Britain on gunsites north and south of the Thames Estuary.

Some of these sites were unpleasant locations, surrounded as they were by the thick muddy tidal waters of the river, by desolate flats and ugly industrial buildings. Some detachments were stationed on barges anchored in the Thames. But for all the unattractive natural surroundings, these outposts were not without some compensations; the ever-changing pageant of the Thames with its swarm of shipping was a constant source of interest to the men guarding its shores. Their chief complaint was that the enemy had now become so shy that they very seldom had a chance of firing their guns.

The first officially recognized Canadian success against an enemy plane was actually achieved by one of the batteries undergoing elementary training at Colchester. In order that the officers and men might have an occasional chance for a shot, it was the nightly custom to deploy detachments from Colchester in gunsites along the neighbouring Essex Coast. One of these detachments, from the 3rd Canadian Light Anti-Aircraft Regiment, while on duty near Frinton on the night of 6-7 August 1941, engaged a Junkers 88. "The third round was observed as a 'hit' and the aircraft caught fire and crashed into the sea". The troop scoring this success had not yet been to practice camp.

During the autumn of 1941, as already observed in Chapter I, the Canadian Corps took over the defence of the Sussex coast. In this forward position they found themselves in the front line of the hit-and-run raids of 1942 and 1943. They suffered no fatal casualties, however, until 11 August 1942, when a bomb landed near the doorway of a shelter in the billet area of a Canadian Field Ambulance stationed at Eastbourne. Eight men were killed and three injured.

During 1942 several successes were scored by Canadian anti-aircraft units in the battle against the hit-and-run raiders. A total of eight enemy aircraft was officially credited to the Canadians; two of these were Focke-Wulf 190's shot down by infantry units. In seven of the eight cases the action took place against enemy sneak raiders attacking towns on the Sussex Coast. In the remaining instance the locale was the Thames Estuary.

These official successes, however, did not make up the full record of action during the year. One incident not included among them, for example, was the work of the 3rd Canadian Light Anti-Aircraft Regiment on Dieppe day, 19 August 1942. Several detachments of this unit accompanied General Roberts' raiding force. At the same time a number of guns were deployed at Bognor Regis to provide protection to the force on its return. During the course of the day these guns destroyed three intruding German aircraft and damaged two; "a good deal of enthusiastic and useful shooting was produced from detachments consisting of drivers and cooks, etc., in the absence of gun crews on the raid". Several bombs were dropped near one of the gun-sites but without causing damage or casualty. Unfortunately, the unit's claims for these successes, while well authenticated by witnesses, were forwarded too late to gain recognition.

Intermittent nuisance raids continued throughout 1943. On 24 May *The Times* reported, "Considerable damage and many casualties were caused when enemy hit-and-run raiders attacked three towns on the south coast early yesterday afternoon". One of the three towns was Hastings, where a Canadian Reconnaissance Regiment—the 17th Duke of York's Royal Canadian Hussars—was stationed. Twelve Focke-Wulf 190's swept in from the sea at roof-top level, spraying the town with bullets as they released their bombs. One of the bombs landed on a hotel housing the men's mess of "A" Squadron and the Y.M.C.A. recreation centre. Fortunately comparatively few men were in the building at the time. Ten were killed, three of them being buried in the debris, and 31 were admitted to hospital. The regiment quickly took hold of the situation and in addition to rescuing its own men assisted the civil defence workers in other parts of the town.

The report of the Y.M.C.A. Supervisor, who was not actually in the canteen at the moment when the bomb fell, gives a vivid impression of the results of such an "incident", and serves also to throw a sidelight on the work of the Canadian Auxiliary Services:

> We immediately began making inquiries as to how many men had been in the centre at the time of the explosion and we were told that two troopers had been playing billiards. The rescue party was put to work at the exact spot where the billiard table had stood and eventually one body was recovered. The other trooper was safe. In all, there were twelve men in the recreation room at the time the bomb fell and all but two escaped unharmed . . . .

The roof was blown completely off our recreation room and two steel beams lay across the floor, but while I was unable to find even a fragment of the billiard-table, the cinema equipment was apparently undamaged . . . . I found out later that the movie projector had been flung twenty feet across the room and buried under piles of rubbish—yet not one of the valves was broken. The tables and chairs were completely unrecognizable, yet a flower vase which was standing on a small table with two flags draped round it was undamaged.

"IN THE WAKE OF THE HUN"

Liverpool, May, 1941. (From a watercolour by Colonel Louis Keene.)

> Some of the men who were there at the time were good friends of the Y, and will be very much missed. Others were seriously hurt but are expected to recover. The morale of all concerned, injured, trapped and rescue parties, was tremendous. One trooper in particular, who had been severely injured, insisted on going on to try and save his friends until he collapsed . . . .
>
> But I can think of nothing that impressed me more than the fact that, two days after the bombing, we had a visit from a deputation of British A.T.S. girls who had been regular visitors to our dances. They brought me along the sum of £11 which they had collected and asked me to use it as I pleased as an expression of their gratitude for all the Y had done for them. Some of this money has already been used to buy cigarettes and chocolate for the men who are now in hospital.

Such were some of the by-products of one piece of German frightfulness.

1943 saw further successes on the part of the Canadian anti-aircraft gunners. On the morning of 23 January five planes attacked Eastbourne, diving low over the town. The leading plane was engaged and shot down by a Bofors team of the 2nd Canadian Light Anti-Aircraft Regiment, Princess Patricia's Canadian Light Infantry sharing in the credit for this victory. A Focke-Wulf 190 which was engaged at the same time crashed into the sea in flames. Again on 3 April and 6 June hits were scored upon raiders over Eastbourne; and on 25 May, when two dozen enemy aircraft swooped on Brighton in daylight, a battery of the 2nd Canadian Heavy Anti-Aircraft Regiment shot down an F.W. 190.

The advent of the flying bomb in the summer of 1944 meant further casualties for Canadian troops stationed in London or near the "bomb highways" in Southern England. Two officers were killed in London when the Guards Chapel at Wellington Barracks was struck during a Sunday morning service in June. In another London incident, in July, when a flat occupied by a group of C.M.H.Q. officers was hit, two batmen were killed and two officers hurt. Several units outside London also had bad luck, the worst instance being that of the Lincoln and Welland Regiment, which suffered nine fatal casualties when one of the bombs burst in their lines in Sussex in July. By the end of July the new German weapon had cost the Canadian Army in the United Kingdom a total of 21 men killed or died of wounds. To men of the Canadian forces in France, the news of the flying bomb offensive had caused much anxiety for friends or families in England. It was a source of deep satisfaction to them when early in September they overran the bomb sites in the Pas de Calais and reduced the menace to minor proportions.

* * * *

It has been ruled by authority that the United Kingdom in this conflict is not and has not been a theatre of operations. Some parts of it have at certain times, however, borne a distinct resemblance to one. When it is considered that nearly 60,000 British civilians have died by enemy action, it may perhaps be conceded that the country, if not a theatre of operations, has certainly been a theatre of war.

For almost five years, the German attacks on Britain were the only form of contact with the enemy vouchsafed to the greater part of the Canadian Army Overseas. The attacks notably failed to break the morale of Britain; and it is certain that they actually helped to maintain the morale of the Canadian troops. The fact that a Canadian unit occasionally came under fire in this way made the long inaction easier to bear; the fact that casualties were suffered now and then—down to 31 July 1944 the Canadian Army lost by enemy action in the United Kingdom nine officers and 107 other ranks killed or died

"DRIFTING DOWN"

Canadian parachutists during an exercise, April, 1944. (From a painting by Capt. G. C. Tinning.) *Two months later this Unit dropped in Normandy on D-Day.*

of wounds, and 22 officers and 254 other ranks wounded—gave the men some sense of nearness to the war which they had crossed the sea to find. It brought them also a keen consciousness of comradeship with and a deep regard for the British people, which no other circumstances could have produced quite so effectively. In this as in other respects the enemy's assault on Britain defeated its own ends. It was designed to destroy the foundations of the Empire; but it left the Empire's forces in better heart, and the Empire's peoples actually more united, more determined, more firmly resolved, than they had been in the days before the first bomb fell.

IV

SAPPERS AT WORK

EVERY arm and service of the Canadian Army had its part to play during the long vigil in Britain in 1940-44, but special reference should be made to the work of the Royal Canadian Engineers. While other branches of the Army were compelled by force of circumstances to fill the necessary but static role of garrison troops, the various engineer units were actively employed in special tasks which carried men of the Corps to all parts of the country from Land's End to John O'Groats and even beyond.

From the beginning of the 18th century, when they were first separated from the artillery by the great Duke of Marlborough, the role of the engineers in warfare has grown steadily more important. One has only to recall the multitude of tasks associated with field defence, bridging, mining, tunnelling and demolitions carried out by Canadian sappers during the last war to realize something of the tremendous responsibilities resting upon this arm of the service under the conditions of modern warfare. To-day it is impossible to mount any large-scale operation without the assistance of the engineers.

A few small Engineer units were included in the Canadian Militia during the early years of the Dominion. It was not, however, until 1903 that the permanent Corps of Royal Canadian Engineers was organized. It has been a source of strength to the war effort of Canada that many forms of military endeavour have had their counterparts in the normal life of the Dominion; and particularly is this true of the engineers. Broadly speak-

PAVING THE RUNWAY

Canadian Engineers at St. Eval, Cornwall, 1943. Liberators of Coastal Command are seen in the background. (From a watercolour by Major C. F. Comfort.)

"DRILLING AT THE BENCH"

Canadian tunnellers at work on a power scheme in Britain.

ing, military and civil requirements in engineer services are not greatly dissimilar. For this reason Canada has been able, during the last war and the present, to mobilize her civilian engineers and rapidly transform them into sappers who have applied to the needs of the army the same energy, resource and enterprise they contributed to the peacetime development of the Dominion.

DRILLING AND TUNNELLING

As the rumblings of war made themselves heard in the uneasy months of 1939, mining engineers and others interested in the mining industry in Canada began to consider the possibility of turning to military advantage the special equipment and techniques developed in Canadian mines. During the summer of 1939 suggestions were made that Canadian mining engineers might visit Europe in order to examine likely fields of battle and report upon the feasibility of diamond-drilling and horizontal boring as offensive expedients against the fortifications of Germany's Siegfried Line.

Immediately following the outbreak of war, Mr. R. A. Bryce, President of the Ontario Mining Association, wrote to the Minister of National Defence (Hon. Norman McL. Rogers), offering to send a commission of Canadian mining engineers to England to study the situation. The Mining Association undertook to bear all preliminary expenses. With this letter he sent a memorandum prepared by a technical committee dealing with the application of civil methods to military needs. Both the Canadian and British Government were interested in the military potentialities of the diamond drill and the pipe-pusher. Among those most active in investigating the practical possibilities of the proposals put forward were General McNaughton, then recently appointed G.O.C. 1st Canadian Division, and Lt.-Col. (later Major-General) C. S. L. Hertzberg. Despite the fact that he was immersed in the task of organizing the division for service overseas, General McNaughton found time to attend at Toronto, on 30 November 1939, a meeting of senior officers, including Lt.-Col. Hertzberg, and representatives of the Canadian mining industry. Here they discussed the possibility of the Royal Canadian Engineers utilizing civilian mining methods and equipment.

It was apparent that much experimental work would have to be carried out before the practicability of diamond-drilling and pipe-pushing for military purposes could be ascertained. General McNaughton therefore proposed that the Hon. Colin A. Campbell, then Minister of Public Works in the Provincial Government of Ontario and a Lieutenant in the 2nd Field Company, R.C.E., should recruit a Special Section of hard-rock miners from northern Ontario and Quebec for this purpose. In the absence of an authorized military establishment the section was to form part of the 12th Field Company, R.C.E., of Winnipeg. It was proposed that the Section should proceed with the 1st Division to Great Britain, where the necessary experiments could be carried out under conditions approximating those which might be expected in France. Should the experiments fail to show encouraging results the section would simply carry on as a normal component of a Field Company of Engineers.

Special equipment was, of course, essential for these experiments; but no funds were available. In order to meet this need the Canadian mining industry organized the War-Time Mining Association and set about raising the necessary money. All mining companies in Canada who were in a position to contribute were invited to do so. From every quarter the response was enthusiastic. Both men and funds were soon available and in January 1940 the soldier miners proceeded overseas with the third flight of Canadian troops.

Upon arrival in England arrangements were concluded with the War Office and the Ministry of Supply for the conduct of experiments in diamond-drilling and horizontal boring. The Special Section was placed directly under the 1st Division's Commanding Royal Engineer, Lt.-Col. Hertzberg; and all personnel were relieved of fatigues and other duties in order to concentrate their full attention upon the work in hand.

The experiments, carried out during the quiet months of the spring of 1940, did much to reveal the military possibilities of the diamond drill and the pipe-pusher. The result was approval for increasing the strength of the Special Section to that of a Tunnelling Company, R.C.E. In May, 1940, the formation of No. 1 Tunnelling Company was authorized.

At this point the War Office, impressed by the success of the Canadian experiments, requested that a detachment of the Canadian Tunnellers might proceed to France for the purpose of preparing signal cable holes which would be invisible to air observation. The rapid and unexpected advance of the German Forces on the Western Front in May and June put an end to this project, just at the moment when all equipment had been packed, motor transport was ready, and the men were on the point of departure. Their disappointment was keen. A few Canadian sappers spent a brief period in France in May surveying the Canadian base area which had been planned near St. Valéry-en-Caux; and some reached Laval during the abortive expedition of June 1940. Later others, like Lance-Sergeant (later Lieutenant) G. A. Hickson, D.C.M, M.M., served gallantly at Dieppe. But for the main body of Royal Canadian Engineers four years were to elapse before they were to land upon the shores of France to breach the defences of Hitler's Atlantic Wall.

During the autumn of 1940 an opportunity of service for which the Canadian Tunnellers were specially qualified presented itself. In the latter part of October a request was received from the British Government that a detachment of hard-rock miners might be sent to Gibraltar. Defensive works of great magnitude and importance were under way on the Rock and trained tunnelling personnel were urgently required. No time was lost. On 11 November approximately one hundred officers and men of No. 1 Tunnelling Company, R.C.E. sailed for Gibraltar—that Rock whose great bulk has stood guard over Great Britain's Mediterranean trade routes for nearly two and a half centuries. In the following spring the 2nd Canadian Tunnelling Company was organized and sent to Gibraltar, where it remained for nearly two years, drilling and blasting out the great subterranean hospital named after the Governor, Field-Marshal Lord Gort, V.C., and extending the labyrinthine tunnels in the heart of the Rock. Not until December 1942 did the Canadian soldier miners and drillers rejoin their comrades in England to fit themselves for their anticipated operational role against the enemy.

BARRING THE GATES

During the critical days of May and June, 1940, when a German landing on the shores of England was an immediate threat, innumerable road-blocks were hastily, and at times haphazardly, erected about the country by various authorities. Many of the blocks built in those feverish weeks were so sited that they would actually have been serious hindrances to the movements of British and Canadian mobile columns operating in a counter-attack role.

Improvisation, however, soon gave way to policy. Steps were taken to prepare defence works on a systematic basis. The general scheme of defence contemplated the construction of a line of anti-tank obstacles extending through the counties south of the Thames, supported by strong points prepared for all-round defence at important airfields and road junctions and distributed over a wide area covering London and other important centres of production and supply. This system of "stops" or strong points was designed to prevent enemy troops who might succeed in establishing a beach-head from running wild and seizing vital points as they had done in France and Belgium.

In the erection of these defences Canadian Engineer units played an important part. At Sarre, a Kentish village at the junction of the roads leading from Margate and Ramsgate, a model fortified village was prepared by No. 1 Pioneer Battalion, R.C.E. When the work was inspected on 12 August, 1940, by Lieutenant-General A. F. A. N. Thorne, G.O.C., 12th Corps and Lieutenant-General McNaughton, then G.O.C. 7th Corps, only a few patches of visible concrete revealed the fact that this village was a strongly fortified position.

At the same time Canadian sappers were employed in strengthening the old fortifications of Chatham, originally constructed by French prisoners of war during the days when Napoleon stood menacingly upon the French shores opposite Dover. Others built pill-boxes and concealed defences, and laid beach mines at vulnerable points overlooking the English Channel from Brighton to Portsmouth. Others again prepared airfields and road junctions for demolition should the enemy obtain a foothold on British soil; while still others were working on anti-tank ditches in the eastern part of Kent.

Much of this work had to be pushed to completion while German bombers were attempting to drive the R.A.F. from the skies and break the British will to resist. While Generals Thorne and McNaughton were visiting Sarre enemy raiders dropped bombs about one hundred and fifty yards from the spot where the two Corps Commanders were standing. There were no military casualties; but the civilian population were not so lucky and the Canadians hastened to their assistance, moving debris and giving first aid. Upon another occasion, near the cathedral town of Canterbury, a German bomber was brought down with Lewis gunfire by two sappers of No. 1 Tunnelling Company, R.C.E. The remainder of the detachment, according to the unit War Diary, "rushed up the hill and celebrated round the burning plane". On 17 August a British driver attached to the same unit was driving a lorry loaded with gelignite through the town of Reigate when an enemy bomb landed only forty yards behind him and several splinters embedded themselves in one of the boxes of explosive. Though badly shaken up, he drove on and did not stop until well clear of the built-up area. It was an action which entailed a high degree of courage as the vehicle might well have exploded.

THE ROAD BUILDERS

It was manifestly impossible at this time to find men and guns in sufficient numbers to hold all coastal defence works in strength. The anti-invasion plans depended for their success upon the rapid movement and concentration of the mobile reserves. But English roads, while beautiful and picturesque, are notoriously narrow and twisty, not least in the towns through which the divisions, with their scores of guns and thousands of vehicles, would have to pass in an emergency. Particularly dangerous, especially in view of the additional hazards of bomb craters and diversions caused by delayed action bombs, were the narrow bottlenecks of Redhill, Reigate, Leatherhead and Lewes.

In view of the grave danger of congestion at these points and the possibility of bombing and "strafing" by enemy aircraft, General McNaughton suggested to the War Office and the Ministry of War Transport that by-pass roads might be constructed around the traffic traps of Redhill and Reigate. He was informed that such a project would require about two-and-a-half years to complete, using civilian labour. The Canadian

G.O.C., however, proposed that the work should be undertaken by the Royal Canadian Engineers. No. 2 Road Construction Company, R.C.E., had recently arrived in England. Of its 350 sappers, many had had extensive road-building experience in Canada; and it was equipped with the latest American-type road building machinery.

Arrangements were finally concluded, and on 3 September 1940 seven huge bulldozers and Letourneau scrapers began pushing down trees and hedges and grading earth for the new by-pass. Within five days the grading had been completed, providing a right-of-way from Nutfield on the Kent road to Salfords on the Brighton road, by-passing Redhill and Reigate. Concreting then began, half a strip being poured at a time in order to maintain a through route for use in emergency. On 19 October the last concrete was poured. In just over six weeks a mile of highway, 22 feet in width, had been constructed, and a mile-and-a-half more of existing roadway widened from 8 to 22 feet.

While the work was in progress the sappers were housed in tents along the right-of-way. This road was located in the vicinity of an R.A.F. airfield and was, moreover, close to the London-Brighton railway; the result was that enemy bombing attacks were frequent. On several occasions the camp was machine-gunned from the air, fortunately without loss to the Canadians. The local anti-aircraft defence, armed with light machine-guns, had many shots at enemy aircraft and claimed a number of hits; but there is no real evidence to show that the road-builders were able to emulate the tunnellers in the actual destruction of an enemy plane.

Beyond the annoyance caused by enemy aircraft and the delays consequent upon the rainy weather, the principal difficulties appear to have arisen from shortage of supplies. Building materials were urgently required for other defence projects such as road-blocks and pill-boxes. The problem of rubble, or hard-core as it is known in England, was finally solved by sending unit convoys to obtain loads from the bombed areas of London. Many a chunk of English history now lies buried beneath the concrete of the Redhill by-pass.

No sooner was the first construction job finished than the next began, namely the by-pass at Leatherhead. This road had already been projected during peacetime but its construction had been postponed owing to the outbreak of war. Since, however, the need for speeding up the movement of military traffic was a paramount consideration the project was revived, and following receipt of the necessary authority from the Ministry of War Transport the Canadians began to move their heavy equipment, tractors and scrapers from Redhill to the new sites.

The scheme as finally agreed upon called for the construction of a 22-foot concrete highway about one-and-a-quarter miles in length linking the two main roads running south and west from Leatherhead.

The technical problems with which the Canadian engineers had to grapple in building this road were knottier than those encountered on the previous job. Not only did the topography present new obstacles (it included a valley with a temperamental river to be bridged and a high railway fill to be underpassed), but the soil in which the work had to be done consisted principally of chalk with a top layer of silty clay, dusty in dry weather and stickier than Canadian gumbo when it was wet. To add to the difficulties, numerous flints in the chalk damaged the blades of the scrapers and cut the tires of the machines.

Although great efforts were made to move dirt during the wet winter months in order to speed construction, they yielded few dividends. More than once work had to be stopped with the tractors bogged down to their bellies in a soil which heavy rain had reduced to a thick milky pudding. And then to make matters still worse the River Mole, normally a quiet little English brook, developed into a raging flood carrying everything in

EXERCISE "PIRATE", OCTOBER, 1943

Landing craft approaching the shore in the first test of the technique later used in the assault on Normandy.

THE PRIME MINISTER OF CANADA OPENS THE LEATHERHEAD BY PASS, AUGUST, 1941

General McNaughton is on Mr. King's left, and at the left of the picture is General Paget, then G.O.C.-in-C., South Eastern Command.

its path downstream. But the job went on; and the road, complete with its bridge and under-pass, was finished in the summer of 1941. The Leatherhead by-pass was officially opened on 28 August by the Prime Minister of Canada.

A point of special interest, in view of subsequent events, should be mentioned here. The construction of these roads helped to bring the bulldozer into its own as an essential item of British military engineering equipment. During the grading of the Leatherhead by-pass a number of tank trials were held at the roadsite by British and Canadian troops; and the bulldozer demonstrated its capabilities by clearing away anti-tank obstacles and assisting tanks at the river crossing. From these trials, in part, developed the armoured bulldozer which was later to play an important role in allied operations in Sicily and Italy and in the Normandy beach-head.

HARNESSING THE WATERS

While some Canadian engineers were helping to gird Great Britain with defensive works and others were building strategic highways, still others were speeding an important power scheme.

A tunnel was undertaken by a civilian contracting firm. But skilled civilian labour was hard to obtain, and the proposal was put forward that a detachment of Canadian hard-rock miners from the Tunnelling Company might be loaned to the contractors to assist in the work. This was agreed to. The Canadians were to drive the tunnel from one end, while a civilian crew worked to meet them from the other.

In order to prevent the work from being flooded it was necessary, first, to construct a temporary adit. A blacksmith-shop, hoist-house, machine-shop, compressor-house, powder-house and other buildings were then erected above the entrance to the shaft, and on 23 April, 1941 the Canadian sappers began driving into the height of land separating them from the civilian crew. The work was carried on twenty-four hours a day, the men working in three shifts.

From the outset there were many problems to solve and difficulties to overcome. The machinery provided for the Canadians was equipment previously used by the civilian drillers. It was old and unfamiliar, and breakdowns led to the loss of many valuable man-hours. Working conditions were not always the best; and on more than one occasion requests were sent to the Tunnelling Company for new men and additional clothing.

At the outset there were complaints about the rations—not of the quality but of the quantity provided. The work was arduous and the men possessed the hearty appetites characteristic of Canadians. After several weeks, thanks to the good offices of the local British Command, extra rations of bread, tea, milk, sugar, meat, jam and butter were obtained for the detachment.

It should perhaps be added that the gamekeepers of the neighbouring estate were apprehensive lest their North American visitors should succumb to the temptation of supplementing the meat ration at the expense of the carefully "preserved" wild life of the district. The occasional sound of a shot echoing through the glens seemed to them to confirm their worst suspicions; but though it is of record that the head gamekeeper spent many hours stalking suspected Canadian poachers, it is likewise of record that he never caught one.

To provide for the leisure time of the men of the lonely detachment was one of the most serious problems. Few people travelled the nearby road and petrol rationing had reduced the number still more. To combat the dangers of boredom, two Nissen huts were constructed at the camp site and a canteen operated by the Navy, Army and Air Force Institutes was set up in one of them, with a reading and writing room in the other. These huts, incidentally, were erected by the men themselves off-shift. The Canadian Auxiliary Services provided musical instruments and moving pictures. An orchestra was formed and dances held weekly, the necessary feminine companions being conveyed by truck from a neighbouring town. There were, of course, occasional breaches of discipline—some of which interfered with the work in hand; generally speaking, however, the conduct of the men was a credit to their corps and to the country from which they came.

Owing to various difficulties the work did not, at first, proceed as quickly as anticipated. The footage achieved by the Canadian sappers was for a time less than that of the civilians drilling to meet them. As the problems were solved, however, the sappers increased their footage; from eighty feet per day in May to one hundred in July and August, and one hundred and ten in October. The record day's drilling was one hundred and forty-two feet achieved on 26 November. This improvement was stimulated partly by the healthy competition of the civilian miners and not least by a bonus for every foot over one hundred, provided by the contractors. And on 15 December "the afternoon shift hit the pilot hole of the tunnel driven from the other end and it was found to be direct centre".

With the task successfully concluded, arrangements were made for the formal completion of the tunnel. Officials of the contracting firm were present together with senior British and Canadian officers. Brigadier C. S. L. Hertzberg, Chief Engineer, Canadian Corps, closed the switch which fired the last charge.

Like many a similar enterprise in peacetime, the Tunnel had taken its toll in human life and had provided the occasion of a display of human heroism.

On 13 June fire broke out in the powder magazine. As he came out of the entrance of the tunnel, Corporal James Hendry noticed the flames. Realizing the grave danger to those working in the nearby shops, he rushed to warn them to take cover. Hendry was an experienced miner; he knew the peril of the situation; and he might easily have escaped injury by sheltering in the tunnel. He did not choose to do so. Having seen the other men safely under cover, he obtained water and made for the magazine to do his utmost to extinguish the fire before the inevitable explosion. Before he reached it the explosion came, and Corporal Hendry met the death which he must have known was all but certain. He was posthumously awarded the second George Cross won by the Canadian Army.

TO KEEP THEM FLYING

1940 and 1941 were the years when Great Britain was on the aerial defensive. By 1942 British and Canadian planes were taking to the air in increasing numbers in raids over the Reich and occupied Europe which formed the prelude to the mighty attacks of 1943 and 1944 against the industries and communications which kept the German military machine in operation. Before this crippling assault could be mounted, however, more and larger airfields were necessary—airfields which could accommodate the growing strength of the British and Allied forces.

It was in April 1942 that the proposal was put forward that the Royal Canadian Engineers should build an airfield at Dunsfold, Surrey, for the use of the Royal Canadian Air Force. The work was to be completed within six months. As it was taking between eleven and twelve months to construct airfields of a similar nature in other parts of England, this was believed by many to be an impossibility.

The project called for the construction of a class "A" bomber field. This included a concrete runway or lane 6,000 feet long and 150 feet wide, two smaller runways 5,200 feet in length, the road encircling the field known as the "taxi track", fifty parking areas and approximately six miles of concrete road through living quarters and administrative area. To accomplish this work it would be necessary to move nearly 100,000 cubic yards of soil; clear, grub and remove stumps from 200 acres of woodland;

excavate drainage and place 130,000 linear feet of drain-pipe; and pour 75,800 cubic yards of concrete (the equivalent of 100 acres of concrete six inches thick). In addition it was necessary to carry out a number of minor jobs not included in the original commitment, such as assisting the electrical contractors to lay cable and erect a lighting system around the airfield.

In order to complete the work within the specified time much planning and organization was necessary. The provision of labour was relatively simple. The bulk of the personnel required was furnished by two Canadian engineer units: the 2nd Battalion, R.C.E., and No. 2 Road Construction Company, R.C.E. To assist them, personnel from other R.C.E. companies including the tunnellers were employed. Units of other branches of the Canadian Army shared in the work: a workshop of the R.C.O.C. and two general transport companies of the R.C.A.S.C., while a company of lumbermen of the Canadian Forestry Corps was brought from Scotland to clear away the great trees which still covered much of the site when the Canadians took it over. Even the Royal Canadian Artillery contributed a gunner to act as assistant paymaster! All told, nearly 2,000 men were employed at the peak period; of these two-thirds worked on the actual construction of the airfield.

Obtaining equipment in sufficient quantities to carry out the work presented several difficulties. Every piece of available machinery in Great Britain, it seemed, was already being utilized in other airfield projects. Fortunately, however, the Canadian engineers were able to supplement their own equipment with machines obtained through the Air Ministry and from a civilian contractor in whose yard were found idle a large concrete-layer and the necessary finishing or levelling machines. These machines formed a part of American Lend-Lease equipment and were, at that time, strange to English workmen, though quite familiar to the Canadian sappers, who had used similar ones in building highways in Canada.

ON THE COAST OF CORNWALL, 1943

Canadian tunnellers quarrying rock for airfield construction.
(From a painting by Major C. F. Comfort.)

⁕ ⁕ ⁕

THE FIRST AIRCRAFT LANDS ON DUNSFOLD AIRFIELD, 20 JUNE 1942

Five weeks earlier, when the Canadian Engineers began work here, the site had been virgin woodland.

The supply of materials, such as cement, crushed gravel, tile drainpipe and even water, also presented a problem. This was, in part, the consequence of a scarcity of the materials in question but it stemmed also from the lack of sufficient transport. When one considers the fact that the project required a daily supply of some 2,000 tons of crushed gravel, 400 tons of Portland cement and over 40,000 gallons of water, it is easy to appreciate the transport difficulties. Nevertheless the job was done, and a word of tribute should be paid to the English civilian women who drove their cumbersome 5-ton trucks with a dexterity and nonchalance which drew words of admiration from every Canadian soldier who watched them.

Work began early in May 1942, when R.C.E. surveyors arrived in Dunsfold with their transits and levels to locate the runways and taxi track. Two weeks later the massive bulldozers began to clear the land. Powder gangs blew out stumps, clearing gangs limbed trees and sawyers converted logs into lumber. Then came the scrapers which levelled the ground and prepared it to receive the concrete surface; and finally the concrete layers, huge machines disgorging nearly 1,000 cubic yards of concrete at a time, moved in to lay the runway.

The men laboured six days a week in two shifts a day, in order to make the most of the available daylight. Shifts alternated weekly, which made possible 48 hours' leave for each man every fortnight.

The R.C.A.F. took a keen interest in the progress of their field. As early as 20 June a two-seater Tiger Moth made a spectacular landing on a short strip of concrete. The machine was brought to a standstill by two sappers holding the wings, the pilot shouting, "Grab a wing, boys, I have no brakes on this rattle-trap". On 28 July Air Marshal Sir Arthur Barratt, R.A.F., with a party of visitors, landed on the runway, made an official inspection and gave a number of the personnel directly connected with the work short flights over the field.

By 15 August, exactly three months and a half from the time the word was given to start work, the runways and taxi track had been completed. This meant that the field could, in emergency, be used at once. Two months later, on 16 October, the Dunsfold Airfield was declared open, when Lieutenant-General McNaughton officially handed it over to Air Marshal H. Edwards of the Royal Canadian Air Force. The undertaking had been accomplished in two weeks under the time-limit originally set.

The ceremony took the form of the unveiling of a commemorative stone in the presence of a guard of honour composed of personnel of the Royal Canadian Engineers and Royal Canadian Air Force. The stone was the gift of an English contractor and the lettering and regimental crests engraved on its face were the work of a Canadian sapper. The ceremony was brought to a conclusion by twelve Canadian Mustangs making a formation landing on the runways. Dunsfold Airfield had ceased to be an airfield in construction and had become another operational field "somewhere in England".

Canadian engineers have worked on other fields. A number of advanced landing grounds have been constructed in England for the Tactical Air Force and work carried out on an airfield in Suffolk and on extensions to an important field in Cornwall.

In April 1943 the Air Ministry made an urgent request for Canadian assistance in reconstructing the airfield at St. Eval, Cornwall, so that it might be used effectively through the following winter by the heavy bombers of Coastal Command operating against enemy U-boats, whose activity had lately been intensified. The project involved building more than 50 dispersal points and extending one of the main runways by 800 feet, which meant laying over 200,000 square yards of concrete. The Canadian Army agreed to furnish the required help, and the 2nd Battalion, R.C.E., was selected for the job. As a certain amount of quarrying was imperative in order to obtain the necessary "aggregate" and wells had to be sunk for water, a detachment of the 2nd Canadian Tunnelling Company was included among the Engineers sent to Cornwall.

As with Dunsfold, the St. Eval extension was an urgent operational necessity and the work was pushed with all speed. It began on 9 June and despite interruptions resulting from heavy rains the job was finished on schedule. On 15 October the completed extension was formally handed over to the Coastal Command by Brigadier J. L. Melville, who congratulated the troops on the speed and efficiency with which they had carried out a task of vital importance in the war against enemy submarines.

Before leaving the subject of airfield construction brief mention might be made of special experiments conducted by the Royal Canadian Engineers on methods of preparing advanced landing grounds. The necessity of finding means for the rapid construction of airfields which without possessing permanent runways would nevertheless be serviceable in wet weather, had been apparent for some time. Indeed the successful exploitation of any bridgehead established in Europe might be imperilled should the necessary air support be lacking through unsatisfactory weather conditions.

Various types of matting or tracking laid out on the ground had been tried, but all had two faults in common: they were not necessary during dry weather and generally unsuccessful during wet periods. Waterproofing dirt runways was tried, experiments along these lines being undertaken by No. 2 Road Construction Company, R.C.E., in the spring of 1943, after Exercise "Spartan" had demonstrated the deficiencies of the method then in use. Different types of surface treatment were tested, none of which proved satisfactory.

The Canadian Engineers then considered the problem from the aspect of preparing a track or runway which could be manufactured in the rear areas, transported to the site selected, and be ready for use soon after it was laid on the ground. Developing this idea one senior officer R.C.E. carried out extensive experiments with pre-fabricated, impregnated hessian and coir in conjunction with surface treatment. Experimental runways of this type were constructed at Dunsfold, and it was found that a full-size runway could be laid in a matter of 16 hours after grading, drainage and consolidation of the field had been completed. These runways were tested during the autumn of 1943 by Mustangs, Typhoons and Spitfires of the R.A.F. The initial defects revealed were quickly overcome and the success of these experiments was such that this method of preparing advanced landing grounds, while not applicable to all conditions, has been widely adopted, not only by the Canadian but also by the British and American Armies. It has been used in France, and also in the Asiatic theatre of operations, where it was introduced by the late Major-General C. S. L. Hertzberg.

THE QUEST FOR STRATEGIC MINERALS

Mining for tin is one of Great Britain's oldest occupations. Even before the Christian Era, Phoenician traders from the Eastern Mediterranean sailed to Britain to obtain cargoes of Cornish tin. In modern times, however, as a result of the development of tin mines in the Orient, Cornwall ceased to be a factor in world production. In Britain tin had to be mined in granite, principally from hard rock 1700 to 1800 feet below the surface of the ground. In Malaya alluvial surface deposits made production on a large scale possible at very low cost.

When the Japanese occupied the Malay peninsula during 1941-42, Great Britain was forced to return to her ancient sources for a metal so essential to the production of arms. The Cornish tin mines had, for the most part, remained disused for half a century, their huge ugly slag heaps standing out as dismal monuments to a decayed industry. It was, however, thought possible to extract some quantities of ore from these mines. Accordingly it was decided to utilize the services of Canadian soldier miners, and various detachments of No. 1 Tunnelling Company were sent to the ancient mines of Cornwall. Here the Canadians carried out exploratory drilling, blasted out new adits and opened up old shafts for the exploitation of remaining deposits.

In addition other groups of tunnellers and drillers assisted the British Ministry of Supply in developing deposits of strategic minerals including fluorspar, hematite, manganese, zinc and wolfram found in various parts of northern England and Wales. Still another party was employed by the British Government on similar work in the far-off Shetland Islands. In August, 1942, No. 1 Special Tunnelling Company had no less than eight separate detachments employed in the search for strategic minerals in various parts of Great Britain.

THE CONSTRUCTORS

Brief mention should be made of the work of the Canadian Artisan Works Companies, formerly known as Construction Companies. As the name implies, these units were formed primarily for building construction purposes and the majority of the personnel were tradesmen, such as bricklayers, plasterers, carpenters and pioneers. At the same time it should be remembered that these men had carried out basic military training and were capable at least of defensive action.

The formation of these units in England was the response to an urgent demand. In the over-crowded island, accommodation for the growing Canadian force, especially in winter, was very hard to find; and civilian labour was so scarce that construction by contract was an extraordinarily slow process. If Canadian camps and hospitals were to be ready when they were needed, Canadians would have to build them.

"ROAD CONSTRUCTION"

A bulldozer at work in England, 1943. (From a watercolour by Capt. O. N. Fisher.)

In the first instance, engineer units of the field army were employed on the most urgent construction jobs, which were mainly new camps required for the Canadian Reinforcement Units and allied establishments in the Aldershot area. Their work enabled accommodation to keep pace with the needs of the steadily increasing Canadian force in the United Kingdom. In due course, special construction units relieved those from the field, which returned to their normal duties. Since that time, constructional activity has been constant. Thanks to the Engineers, the accommodation provided for the Canadians—hutted camps, hospitals, depots and workshops—has compared favourably with that occupied by any other element of the vast Allied force which was built up in the island in preparation for the invasion of Europe.

* * * *

War is not all destruction. As the Prime Minister of Canada remarked in opening the Leatherhead by-pass, it often brings in its train constructive effort as well; sometimes with permanent benefit to mankind. In a sense, the continuance of British civilization is itself the monument to the men of many lands who gathered in the British Isles to defend freedom's cause, and went out from the islands to lay down their lives for it on many battlefields. But the Canadian Engineers who worked in Britain have left more material memorials of themselves. The defences with which they helped to girdle the coasts will doubtless vanish as better days return; but here and there some parts of the work they did will continue to serve future generations of Britons. English traffic will long roll over roads built by Canadian sappers; airfields on which the Canadians worked may serve the transports of peace as well as the bombers of war; and the mineral deposits explored by the tunnellers from the Dominion may make a palpable contribution to the prosperity as well as the security of the British Isles.

V

A LITTLE BEHIND THE FRONT

A MODERN army is a tremendously complex organization. Ever since warfare developed beyond the phase of single combat the importance of the rearward services has steadily increased. Thus the record of the field army, its development, defensive role and sorties beyond the walls of the citadel during the years 1940 to 1944, is only part of the story of the Canadian troops in Britain. Behind the field army, and auxiliary or supplementary to it, were establishments of many different services without which it could not have carried on under modern conditions of warfare. It is impossible to do justice to all these services here; this chapter must, therefore, confine itself to explaining only a few of the more important activities of the Canadian troops "behind the lines".

The static establishments in Britain were, and are, under the command and direction of Canadian Military Headquarters, London, which thus relieved the field command of responsibility for such matters and leaves it free to concentrate on the business of beating the enemy. During the first months of the war, as we have seen, the appointment of Senior Officer at these headquarters was held by Major-General (later General) H. D. G. Crerar. On his return to Ottawa to become Chief of the General Staff, the appointment passed to Major-General (later Lieut.-General) the Hon. P. J. Montague, who held it until the command arrangements at C.M.H.Q. were reorganized in December, 1943. Lieutenant-General K. Stuart then took up the new appointment of Chief of Staff there; and General Montague became Major-General in Charge of Administration.

THE REINFORCEMENT UNITS

In order that the overseas divisions of the Canadian Army might at all times be kept up to fighting strength it was essential that there should be a continuous flow of men from Canada as well as a considerable body of trained reinforcements always ready in England. The numbers despatched overseas were not based upon the vagaries or hazards of recruiting, but upon careful estimates of the officers and men likely to be required during periods of normal or intense activity as demonstrated by actual experience in the field. At the beginning of the war this estimate was based upon the calculations of 1914-18, with such modifications as might reasonably be expected in view of development of new weapons and changed conditions of warfare.

The volunteer offering himself for active service received his initial training at one or other of the Basic and Advanced Training Centres organized in the Dominion during the summer of 1940. After varying periods, depending upon the requirements of the field army and the length of time required for training in the different branches, he was sent overseas as a member of a reinforcement draft. On arrival in England he was posted to a Holding Unit according to his particular arm or service. During the spring of 1940 steps were taken to organize six reinforcement Holding Units for the 1st Canadian Division.

With the fall of France it became obvious that the role of the Canadian troops overseas would be, for some time to come, defensive in character, and that the number of reinforcements required would probably be less than originally anticipated. It did not follow, however, that Canadian reinforcements should be reduced to conform to the British scale for "quiet" periods. The threat of invasion loomed over England and the Canadians, far from their home depots, could not, like the British units, be rapidly reinforced.

The despatch of additional Canadian formations overseas led naturally to an increase in the number and importance of the Reinforcement Holding Units. In September 1940 three Groups were formed in the Aldershot area, each comprising several Holding Units organized according to arms and services. These Groups, whose strength along with other Canadian units in the area was not far short of that of a division in the field, were placed under Brigadier (later Major-General) L. F. Page, who at an earlier time had commanded the Canadians in Iceland. Subsequently Brigadier (later Major-General) F. R. Phelan assumed the command.

During 1941 and 1942 the growing strength of the Canadian Army Overseas necessitated the formation of additional Groups, until the size and importance of the reinforcements units were such that they became a Major-General's responsibility. In April 1943, Major-General J. H. Roberts, who had previously commanded the 2nd Canadian Division, was appointed to command the Canadian Reinforcement Units.

As at October, 1944, the Canadian Reinforcement Units consisted of six Groups, lettered from "A" to "F", each commanded by a Brigadier. "A" and "D" Groups consisted of the various Infantry Reinforcement Units, or C.I.R.Us. as they are called; "B" Group included Engineer, Signals and Army Service Corps units; "C" Group, two Artillery units and an Ordnance unit; "E" Group, three Armoured units or C.A.C.R.Us.; and "F" Group, all special static units. Broadly speaking, reinforcements for the infantry are organized as far as possible on a territorial basis, that is, by provinces and regions of Canada.

In order to ensure an adequate supply of trained reinforcements, officers and men, qualified to take their place in the fighting line, it was necessary to organize special training establishments additional or supplementary to the Reinforcement Units. To provide staff officers the Canadian Junior War Staff Course was set up in England in the autumn of 1940. Subsequently this course was transferred to the Royal Military College at Kingston, Ontario. Another organization was the Canadian Training School, whose various wings give specialized instruction in different branches. One of these is the Battle Wing, which teaches the new battle drill technique already described; another was the Officer Cadet Training Unit whose business it was to train candidates for commissions. This unit for a long period gave at least part of their training to all Canadian overseas cadets; subsequently, however, the policy was adopted of returning cadets to Canada for training, and more recently arrangements have been concluded with the British authorities whereby Canadian cadets selected from the Army Overseas will receive their training in British establishments after a preliminary course at a Canadian School. Another wing of the School trained Canadians, before D-Day, in the use of the flame-throwers which have since struck terror into the Germans in France and the Low Countries.

Although their primary function was to train and hold officers and men in readiness to take their place in the battle line, the Canadian Reinforcement Units were also required to assume some responsibility for the defence of Great Britain in the event of enemy invasion. This "operational role" was principally local in character. It consisted of providing mobile columns to combat enemy parachutists, manning the defences of Bordon and Witley and various road-blocks in conjunction with the Home Guard, and finding guards for vulnerable points such as aerodromes, landing grounds and wireless stations. Training exercises were carried out to practise the men in the tasks which they might be called upon to perform should the enemy actually succeed in gaining a foothold upon British soil.

After the defence of the Sussex Coast became a Canadian responsibility, men of the Reinforcement Units were, from time to time, called upon to share it. When units of the field army were withdrawn from their forward positions in order to participate in the great collective exercises of 1942 and 1943, selected troops of the Reinforcement Units were sent to Sussex to guard the vital coastal areas. During Exercise "Tiger" in May 1942, a special force known as "Wolf Force", consisting of nine battalions and commanded by Brigadier Phelan, was deployed to cover the positions normally held by the units of the 1st Canadian Corps. In the following year during Exercise "Spartan" a similar force was organized for the same purpose.

The question may be asked why so many reinforcements were required while active Canadian operations were confined to relatively minor affairs. Such a query is based upon the assumption that the number required would be confined to normal wastage and accidents causing medical unfitness. It should be remembered that even during quiet periods there was a constant drain upon the available manpower overseas. In addition to those who were discharged for medical reasons (and there were inevitably some men who were unable to stand the increasingly heavy strain imposed by training for modern warfare), there were demands upon the reinforcement reservoir for men to complete revised establishments or fill new units which have been formed as a result of the battle experience gained by British troops in other theatres of war. It was always necessary to maintain provision against the possible sudden outbreak of active operations. And today, with formations of the Canadian Army in the front line of battle on two European fronts, the need for replacements continues constant and imperative. The reserves must be kept up.

SCOTTISH FORESTS AND CANADIAN FORESTERS

Wood is an indispensable munition of war. It is required for buildings, for ammunition boxes, for railway sleepers and pit props. Plywood is needed for aeroplanes and boat skins. By-products of wood are equally if not more essential for war purposes. Paper goes into everything from shellcases to films; alcohol is required for explosives and rubber, and plastics may be used for innumerable purposes.

During the last war Great Britain was faced with a shortage of this vital material. Unable to find the necessary shipping to import greater quantities of lumber from Canada, the Secretary of State for the Colonies requested the Dominion to send overseas a battalion of lumbermen to work in the woods of Britain and France and thus ease the situation by increasing home production. As early as May 1916 this battalion was producing sawn lumber in England, and in October 1916 the Canadian Forestry Corps was authorized.

Before the end of hostilities in 1918 the Corps had extended its operations from Southampton to Inverness and from Bordeaux to the Jura Mountains. The total strength, including attached labour, amounted to 31,447 all ranks in November 1918: while production to the end of that year totalled 813,541,560 board feet. It is a fact that "over 70 per cent of the total timber used by the Allied Armies on the Western Front was supplied by the Canadian Forestry Corps".

With this achievement in mind, the Right Hon. Anthony Eden, Secretary of State for the Dominions, approached the Canadian Government in 1939 to learn if Canada would be prepared to despatch Forestry units to Great Britain and France under arrangements similar to those of the last war. The successes which attended the German onslaughts in Scandinavia and the Low Countries in the spring of 1940, together with the increasing intensity of the Battle of the Atlantic and the heavy demands upon shipping for the Middle East and other theatres of war, constituted a state of affairs not dissimilar from that which had led to the formation of the original Forestry Corps in 1916. More than ever it became essential to increase British home

SCOTLAND, 1942

Men of the Canadian Forestry Corps march past the Minister of National Defence at the Headquarters of the Corps.

SEPTEMBER, 1942

Men of a Canadian artillery reinforcements unit manning a 25-pounder on the range.

SCOTLAND, 1943

Two "fallers" of a Canadian Forestry Company bring down a tree.

"JAMMER LOADING LOGS"

Canadian Forestry Corps, Scotland. (From a watercolour by Capt. W. A. Ogilvie.)

production of sawn lumber. And with their experience of lumbering, their up-to-date methods and machines, Canadians appeared to the British Government to be the men to make the most of the British timber reserves.

The Dominion agreed to provide twenty Companies for overseas service; and in July 1940 the Canadian Forestry Corps was organized under the command of Brigadier (later Major-General) J. B. White, D.S.O., E.D., who had commanded the Canadian Forestry Corps in France during the last war. Recruiting for the Corps was carried on during the summer and autumn. In October the advance party left Canada for Scotland and, two months later, the first Canadian Forestry Company, one recruited at the Head of the Lakes, landed at Gourock.

Arrangements for equipment and timber limits were made with the War Office and the Ministry of Supply by Canadian Military Headquarters. In view of the fact that these companies were formed at the specific request of the British Government and for British purposes, the cost of maintaining the Corps was to be shared by the two governments. The Dominion assumed responsibility for pay and cost of transportation to and from Great Britain, while all expenses incurred in connection with technical equipment and maintenance were to be paid by the United Kingdom.

Scarcely had the first companies been despatched when the suggestion was put forward by the Secretary of State for the Dominions that the number of companies overseas might be increased. This the Canadian Government agreed to do. Additional units were sent to Scotland during the course of 1941 and 1942, until finally a total of thirty Canadian Forestry Companies were engaged in lumbering operations over a wide area of the Scottish Highlands, reaching almost from Loch Shin to the River Tay.

The various companies were recruited from all parts of the Dominion; from the Rocky Mountains to the Great Lakes; from Quebec to the Maritimes; and even from the allegedly treeless Prairies. Many were veterans of the last war. As in the case of the engineer units, a large number of the men who enlisted were employed in the Corps in the same jobs which they had filled in civilian life, as sawyers, mill operators, storemen, loggers, cooks or mechanics. Some of them came from the big pulp and paper companies of Eastern Canada; others from the small semi-portable mills to be found in all parts of the Dominion; still others were without experience of lumbering of any kind and looked upon the Corps as a new adventure.

The operational unit of the Corps was the Forestry Company, a unit designed to carry out two complementary jobs: cutting the timber in the bush, and sawing it into lumber in the mill. It had a normal establishment of six officers and 188 other ranks. The thirty companies were grouped under five Administrative Districts, each commanded by a Lieutenant-Colonel. These Districts were arranged on a geographical basis and were not uniform in the number of companies they contained. The whole organization was administered by a Corps Headquarters located at Beauly near Inverness, hard by the seat of the famous Highland house of Lovat. Although the Forestry Corps came under the technical direction of the Home Grown Timber Production Department of the Ministry of Supply, for all military operational and administrative purposes it remained under the command of Canadian Military Headquarters.

The Corps attained its maximum strength during the first six months of 1943. On 31 July 1943 personnel of the Corps totalled 224 officers and 6,385 other ranks.

It is not unworthy of note that the present Forestry Corps is a combatant formation. Not only were the officers and men, for the most part, experienced lumbermen, they were also trained soldiers. The majority of the senior officers were either veterans of the last war or members of the Non-Permanent Active Militia. All ranks were required to undergo two months basic training in Canada. This training was continued overseas. Five days a week the men felled, sawed and transported lumber. On Saturdays they donned battle dress and web equipment and engaged in drill, musketry and tactical exercises. The Forestry Corps is armed with modern infantry weapons and has been allotted a definite operational role in the defence of Scotland in conjunction with the regular troops of Scottish Command and the local Home Guard.

In the spring of 1943 the proposal was put forward that the units of the Canadian Forestry Corps might, without handicap to the war effort of the Empire, be reduced in number in order to make additional manpower available for the field army. Several months later the Canadian Government officially announced that a portion of the Corps would be returned to Canada to work in Canadian woods. It was apparent that the time was rapidly approaching when some change in the disposition of the Corps would be necessary owing to the smaller stands of timber available in Scotland. With the U-boat menace largely overcome by the joint efforts of the Navy and the Air Force, the sea-transport situation was eased; while it was possible with the same effort to produce a greater output of large timber in Canada than in the United Kingdom. Moreover the by-products of an expanded lumber industry might help to alleviate the fuel shortage in the Dominion. During October ten companies and one District Headquarters embarked for Canada.

At the same time that preparations were in hand to reduce the Canadian Forestry commitment in the United Kingdom, however, arrangements were being made for the allocation of ten companies and a District Headquarters to the 21st Army Group for employment in France with the field army. These men were given refresher training in anticipation of their early employment in the theatre of war. The remaining ten companies have carried on with logging and milling operations in the Highlands.

The daily average output of the various Canadian Forestry Companies in Scotland has totalled approximately 22,000 to 26,000 board feet. Sawn lumber constitutes the main contribution of the Corps. In addition, pit props, pulp wood, slab wood, telegraph poles and boat skins are all part of the production of each individual company in varying quantities according to the type of timber worked. Figures to the end of December 1943 show a total output of sawn lumber for the "national stock" of 314,500,730 f.b.m., with 162,760 tons of tonnage wood, 26,882 tons of pulp wood.

The Canadian foresters have been employed in other tasks besides their primary ones of felling, trimming and sawing trees. Mills and bunkhouses have been erected. In winter, the Canadians have helped to keep the Scottish roads open, using snow ploughs mounted on trucks and tractors. Personnel of the Corps have worked as fire fighters; assisted other Dominion Forestry troops; built a large prisoner-of-war camp; and helped to clear the great airfield at Dunsfold. There are no more versatile men in the Canadian Army than those of the Forestry Corps. They are willing to turn their hands to anything; and those who know them best say that the jobs they do turn their hands to are invariably well done.

UNDER THE GENEVA CROSS

Care for the sick and wounded in war has been a comparatively modern development. Even as late as the middle of the 19th century, army medical services were inadequate and, in some instances, practically non-existent. It was the revelation of the horrible conditions in the Crimea which led Florence

Nightingale and her band of nurses to leave England to tend the casualties in the fever-ridden hospitals at Scutari. Out of her exertions came the complete reorganization of the Army Medical Services and the institution of nursing as an essential part of those services.

The first distinctively Canadian Medical Service was that improvised in 1885 by Surgeon-General D. Bergin and Sir Thomas Roddick at the time of the North-West Rebellion. In 1899 a special department was created with a Director-General at its head. During the war of 1914-18 the Canadian Medical Services, drawing upon the resources of the civilian profession, established a very high standard of organization and professional skill. At the conclusion of hostilities, however, the permanent Corps was reduced to a strength sufficient only to meet the needs of the Permanent Force. When the war broke out in September 1939, only a very limited army medical service existed in Canada. The permanent strength numbered but forty-two officers and eleven nursing sisters. There were, however, a number of Field Ambulances, Casualty Clearing Stations, Field Hygiene Sections, and eighteen reserve General Hospitals in the Non-Permanent Active Militia. Some of these units, such as the field ambulances, underwent brief periods of training at the annual summer camps with other militia units; others, like the reserve general hospitals, existed only as cadres on paper.

From this nucleus developed the large, well-equipped, efficiently-staffed medical organization of the Canadian Army Overseas. At the present time there are approximately two hundred different medical units overseas. These include twenty-four General Hospitals, eleven Field Ambulances, five Casualty Clearing Stations, three Convalescent Hospitals, five Medical Stores Depots, and a wide variety of units such as Field Surgical Units, Field Transfusion Units, Mobile Hygiene Laboratories, and Mobile Neuro-Surgical Units. A number of these units, including five General Hospitals and five Anti-Malarial Control Units, are serving the Canadian troops in the Mediterranean area.

The premises occupied at different times by the various Canadian hospital units in England have included former British military hospital establishments like the Connaught Hospital at Aldershot, and civilian hospital buildings such as those occupied at Watford near London, and Marston Green, near Birmingham. In other instances buildings have been especially erected to house Canadian hospitals. Notable among the latter category is the hospital near Taplow, Bucks.

During the war of 1914-18 a Canadian hospital had been built at Cliveden, the beautiful Thames-side estate of the Astor family. This, known as No. 15 Canadian General (Duchess of Connaught's) Hospital, was opened in March 1915 and functioned usefully until the end of the war. At the outset of hostilities in 1939 Lord and Lady Astor once more offered part of their property to the Canadian Red Cross Society for hospital purposes. According to the terms of the agreement the property was turned over to the Society "for the duration of the present war or until the actual cessation of hostilities by Great Britain . . . and further until determined by either party giving to the other at least three calendar months' notice". The annual rent payable was to be one shilling! The old buildings of the last war were no longer standing and new ones were erected during the spring of 1940, the cost being borne by the Canadian Red Cross Society, which also undertook to furnish the hospital with ordnance equipment on the regulation military scale. The Canadian Government provided the necessary medical and technical supplies. On 15 July the hospital was officially opened by the Rt. Hon. R. B. (later Viscount) Bennett, who turned it over to the High Commissioner for Canada, the Rt. Hon. Vincent

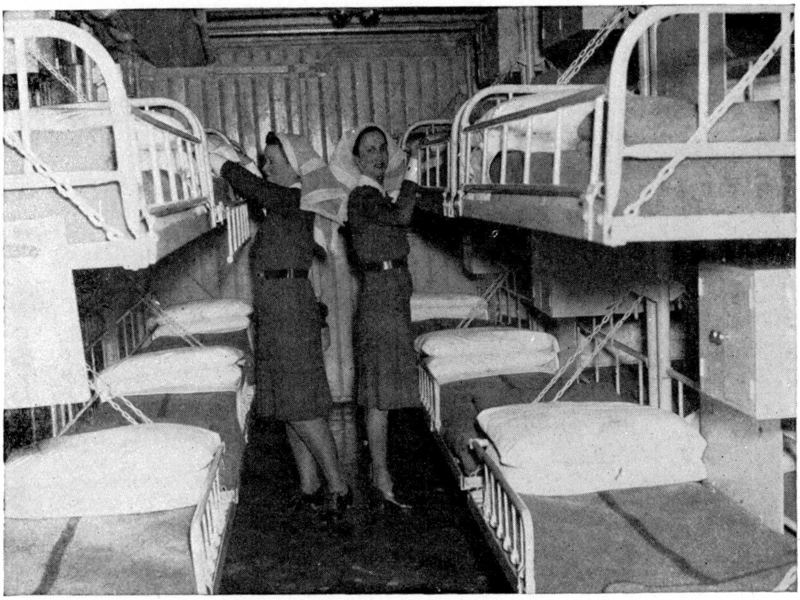

Two Nursing Sisters of the R.C.A.M.C. in a Ward of the Hospital Ship "Lady Nelson".

The Entrance to Taplor Hospital, on the Astor Estate, which has Housed Canadian Hospitals in Two Wars.

"CASUALTY GOING ABOARD HOSPITAL CARRIER"

Combined Operations training in Scotland, 1943. (From a pen and watercolour drawing by Capt. W. A. Ogilvie.)

CANADIAN HOSPITAL SHIP

The "Lady Nelson" at a British Port after bringing casualties from the Mediterranean, 1943.

Massey, for the use of the Royal Canadian Army Medical Corps. Nine days later the first patient was admitted. The Taplow Hospital, which has been staffed at different times by members of Nos. 5, 7 and 11 Canadian General Hospitals, was the first Canadian military hospital to function overseas during the present war.

It is obviously impossible to mention every hospital; one other besides Taplow should, however, be noted. Early in 1940 a 200-bed field hospital was mobilized in Canada with the primary purpose of treating head injuries and battle neuroses near the forward area. Owing to the collapse of France while this hospital was on its way overseas, it was settled in England at Hackwood Park near Basingstoke. The property belonged to Lord Camrose and had been leased for the duration of the war by the British Ministry of Health. The hospital grew in bed space and personnel until in July 1943 it reached its present status as a 600-bed hospital. Of this number 150 beds have been set aside for a Plastic Surgery Unit. Considerable progress has, meanwhile, been made in the dissemination and standardization of knowledge of military neuropsychiatry, and medical officers from the various general hospitals have been attached for periods of one to three months to the Basingstoke Neurological and Plastic Surgery Hospital.

To deal adequately with the work of the Royal Canadian Army Medical Corps during the years 1940-44 would require a volume rather than a few paragraphs. Here we can give but a brief outline of the great services of the Corps. Despite the long period of quiet the medical units were far from idle. The prevention of disease is as important if not more important than the actual treatment of casualties, and the medical services have devoted their attention to a multitude of tasks in connection with field hygiene, inoculations and vaccinations, tuberculosis and venereal disease control, and dozens of other activities.

It was not until the raid on Dieppe in August 1942 that the Canadian medical services were faced with the problem of dealing with battle casualties. That event suddenly plunged the hospitals in England into the conditions of active operations. Despite the fact that, for reasons of security, no advance information of the raid was given to the Director of Medical Services until the actual morning on which it took place, effective arrangements were instantly put in hand to receive and treat the wounded as they returned. Casualties were evacuated from ports to various Canadian General Hospitals; special trains were arranged to transport them; a plastic surgery team was ready at Basingstoke. All arrangements functioned smoothly and efficiently. Approximately 600 casualties, mostly Canadian, were treated in Canadian hospitals. Of these less than three per cent died after admission; thirty per cent of the cases were discharged within two weeks.

Preparations were made in England well in advance to deal with the casualties which it was anticipated would follow the assault upon Hitler's Atlantic Wall. On 6 June 1944 the day of trial was at hand. During the assault phase, three Canadian General Hospitals acted in the capacity of transit hospitals, taking large numbers of casualties direct from the ports, operating on the more seriously injured, and sending the minor cases by train to other hospitals. The hospitals have continued to carry a heavy burden in later phases, and have lived up splendidly to the military and professional traditions of the R.C.A.M.C. The surgery has been of the highest standard and the mortality gratifyingly low.

An item of special interest has been the fitting out of two hospital ships for Canadian troops. As early as 1941 the suggestion was made that Canada might have her own vessel to convey wounded Canadian soldiers from the theatre of war to hospitals at home. This proposal was finally realized in the spring of 1943, when the Canadian National Steamship "Lady Nelson", which had been torpedoed at Barbados and was lying half-submerged in mud at Mobile, Alabama, was refloated and fitted out to be a Canadian hospital ship. On 6 May 1943 the embarkation of invalids took place at a British port and on the morning of the 7th the vessel set sail for Canada on her maiden voyage as a hospital ship. She carried not only 316 sick and wounded Canadians but also 144 American casualties from North Africa. Since that date she has been constantly in service bearing Canadian, British and American soldiers from the Mediterranean area to Great Britain and Canada. She has also carried wounded German prisoners of war for repatriation from Canada to England. More recently a second vessel, the S.S. "Letitia", has been fitted out for hospital purposes and will be used to carry casualties across the North Atlantic.

Finally, a special word of tribute should be paid to the Canadian Red Cross Society. Through the efforts of this voluntary organization many articles of an essential nature have been supplied to Canadian hospitals in England and elsewhere, including blood plasma, garments, bandages, books, games, and radio sets. Wherever Canadian soldiers are fighting the workers of the Canadian Red Cross will be found close at hand ready to bring comfort to them when they are wounded or ill.

YOUNG LADIES IN KHAKI

On 26 June 1941 the Canadian Government formally announced its decision to form women's auxiliaries for the Canadian Army and the Royal Canadian Air Force. A month and a half later, on 13 August, the Canadian Women's Army Corps was authorized by Order-in-Council, and formed as an ancillary to the Canadian Active Army under the Department of National Defence. The women of Canada were able to take their place side by side with their fathers, husbands and brothers in the armed services.

As early as 1938 women in Canada had begun to make preparations to do their share in the event of hostilities. In November 1939 they voluntarily registered their qualifications for national service. This was followed in July 1940 by the National Registration of all man- and woman-power in Canada. There appeared to be no immediate need to utilize the potential reserve thus revealed and no official action was taken to organize Canadian women for war services at this time.

In view of the fact that British women had been enrolled in a variety of official and semi-official organizations, many Canadian women felt it appropriate that they should be given similar opportunities for service. Accordingly they started in various parts of the Dominion voluntary organizations at which courses in such subjects as physical training, motor mechanics, first aid, home nursing and office administration were given. By November 1940 almost 17,000 women were enrolled in such organizations throughout Canada, and these organizations did much to prepare the way for official action.

The demands upon Canada's available manpower for the armed services, war industries, agriculture and other essential occupations steadily increased as the war went on; and in 1941 the Canadian Government resolved to enrol several thousand women volunteers for active Army service in Canada on a full-time basis. It was proposed to employ these women as cooks, clerks, stenographers and telephone operators, and thus release men from these occupations for combat service. Such was the origin of the C.W.A.C.

The response to the appeal for volunteers was, in the words of the Minister of National War Services, "magnificent". On 1 September the first recruits reported for duty; and on 23 February 1942 the first course for Officers and N.C.Os. began at Ste.

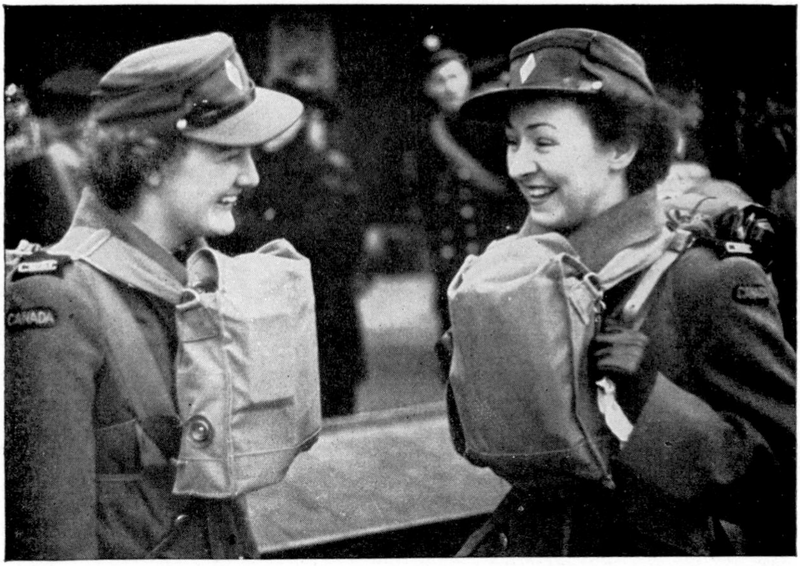

THE C.W.A.C. COMES TO BRITAIN

Two girls of the first contingent on the quay after landing, 5th November, 1942.

LONDON, 1944

Two C.W.A.C. drivers of Canadian Military Headquarters cleaning up a staff car.

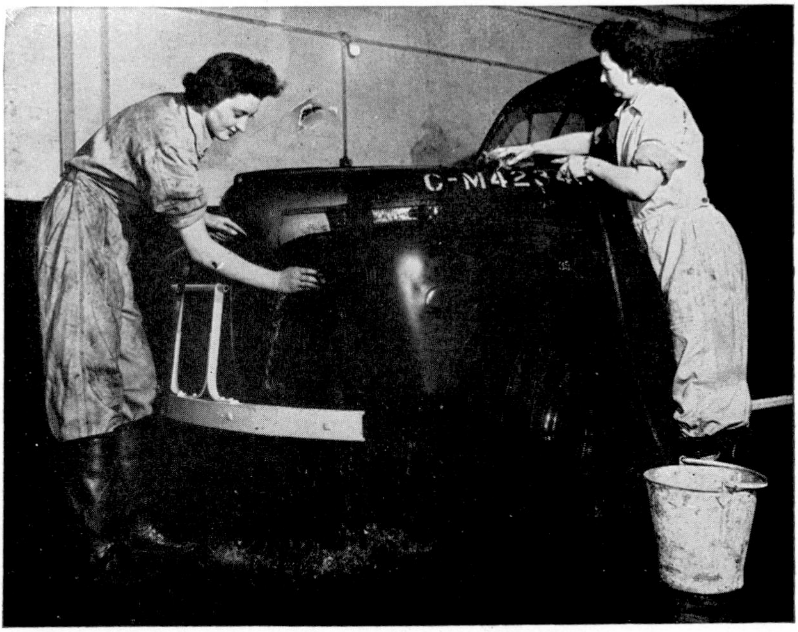

Anne de Bellevue. In March the Corps was promoted from auxiliary to full army status. With this recognition the C.W.A.C. became "a Corps of the Active Militia of Canada" and its members were placed "on active service" on the same basis as men.

It had not originally been intended that the C.W.A.C. should be employed beyond the limits of the Dominion. The change in this policy arose in the first instance out of the need to find personnel to operate a Static Base Laundry which it was proposed to establish in England to serve Canadian troops. In similar British establishments Auxiliary Territorial Service girls were employed; and since the British authorities made it clear that civilian labour would not be available, the most suitable alternative appeared to be the employment of Canadian women. Early in 1942, accordingly, the proposal was sent to Ottawa that 150 C.W.A.C. personnel trained in laundry work might be sent to Great Britain.

Once the principle of overseas service for Canadian women had been accepted it was a short step to the enlargement of their spheres of employment. A survey was undertaken at Canadian Military Headquarters during the spring of 1942 with a view to ascertaining how many "A" category male personnel might be released for service in the field army by utilizing the services of the C.W.A.C. as clerks and stenographers. Finally, on 5 November, 104 C.W.A.C. personnel arrived in the United Kingdom. Within a few days a large number of them had been taken into employment in the various branches of Canadian Military Headquarters and were learning the duties which they were to take over from soldier clerks who in due course moved to units in the field.

Arrangements had already been made with the British Ministry of Works for suitable barracks for the girls in London; and the buildings requisitioned were altered, repaired and decorated to meet the needs of the new arrivals. Central heating was installed, air raid shelters erected and other improvements made. The Canadian Auxiliary Services furnished pianos, radios, card tables, writing tables and sundry games.

Excited, happy and delighted with their quarters, the first arrivals were given an enthusiastic welcome. Particularly pleased to greet them were Canadian soldiers who had not seen Canadian girls for two and three years. It is recorded that the one telephone in the original barracks was greatly over-worked as the girls endeavoured to establish communication with husbands, relatives and friends. They rapidly acclimatized themselves; although the blackout remained a source of difficulty to those unacquainted with the irregularities and sinuosities of London streets.

The second group of C.W.A.C. personnel numbering 141 all ranks, arrived in England on 19 December 1942; and the third and fourth groups in the following March and May. The first three drafts were organized on a company basis, and were numbered 41, 42 and 43 in order of arrival overseas. A fifth group, subsequently known as No. 47 Company, arrived during May 1943 and was allotted to Headquarters, Canadian Reinforcement Units. In July the long-awaited laundry draft reached the United Kingdom. Further drafts arrived during 1944 and a fifth Company, No. 50, was organized. Eighteen months after the arrival of the first draft in England, the overseas strength of the Corps reached a total of 67 officers and 964 other ranks.

Owing to the number of applications which had been received from Canadian women resident overseas, arrangements were made to enlist them into the Corps. The practice adopted was similar to that followed in the case of men enlisted into the Canadian Army in England; enrolment being limited to those who could claim to be Canadian nationals by birth, marriage or domicile. On 19 February 1943 General Montague took the salute at the passing-out parade of the first group of C.W.A.Cs.

enlisted and trained in Great Britain. By the end of 1944 over 200 recruits have been enrolled in the United Kingdom; of these over 50 were former members of the Auxiliary Territorial Service.

Although officers have naturally been sent overseas from Canada, arrangements have also been made for the training of C.W.A.C. personnel in England for commissions. After an initial recommendation and examination by Personnel Selection, candidates are sent to an Auxiliary Territorial Service Training School to complete their qualification. On 2 April 1943 the first group of C.W.A.C. cadets received their certificates of graduation from the G.O.C.-in-C., First Canadian Army. Provision has also been made for the mutual exchange of officers between the C.W.A.C. and the A.T.S. for three-month periods of attachment in Great Britain and Canada.

There was an important new departure in the spring of 1944. The employment of Canadian women in the rear areas of theatres of war had not been envisaged when the Corps was organized in 1941; but three years later the shortage of manpower was becoming acute. It was accordingly proposed that C.W.A.C. personnel might be employed in the Canadian administrative headquarters in Italy and in France in capacities similar to those of the A.T.S. in corresponding British establishments. The matter was referred to National Defence Headquarters, and permission was granted in April 1944.

Late in May the first detachment, consisting of one officer and 17 other ranks, left England to serve with Canadian Section, G.H.Q. 1st Echelon, the Canadian static headquarters in Italy. A small number of C.W.A.Cs. are now employed at Supreme Headquarters, Allied Expeditionary Force, and a large number at Canadian 1st Echelon, 21st Army Group. Authority has also been granted for the posting of C.W.A.C. personnel to 2nd Echelon, 21st Army Group. Canadian women, accordingly, are

CANADIAN SOLDIERS VISITING H.M.S. "VICTORY" (From a watercolour by Major C. F. Comfort.)

now serving in North-West Europe as well as in the Mediterranean area.

The young women of the C.W.A.C. are performing a great variety of services in the Canadian Army Overseas. The majority are serving in clerical capacities, as clerks, stenographers, and typists. Others are employed as cooks, switchboard operators, cipher operators, dental assistants, postal sorters, and drivers. One woman is employed as a technical draftsman. Approximately 390 are general duty personnel; this includes those employed at the Static Base Laundry. Others, members of the concert parties of the Canadian Army Show, have not only visited Canadian troops stationed in various parts of Britain, but have also journeyed to Italy and France to entertain the men in the theatres of war. To say that their presence there has been vastly appreciated is to put it very mildly.

Officers of the C.W.A.C. are to an increasing degree undertaking staff work at static headquarters, thus freeing young male staff officers for service in the field. There are many staff appointments which C.W.A.C. officers can fill very satisfactorily after appropriate training. A number of such officers have already taken the A.T.S. Staff Course and distinguished themselves in it.

Of the many innovations that this war has brought to the Canadian Army, the organization of the Canadian Women's Army Corps is one of the most completely successful. It was doubtless not undertaken without misgivings, and some old-fashioned soldiers were certainly heard to mutter prophecies of failure. Their fears proved wholly groundless, and today the C.W.A.C. has proved itself as not the least valuable element in the complex fabric of the Canadian Army Overseas.

VI

THE CANADIANS AND THE BRITISH PEOPLE

THIS little book, it was said in the beginning, describes an episode unique in British history. Never before had a great section of the population of one of the Dominions been picked up bodily, as it were, and set down to dwell in the Mother Country for a period of years. The last war was no parallel, for at that time the United Kingdom had been for the men of the Canadian Corps not much more than a way-station on the route to France. Now, however, between two and three hundred thousand Canadians found themselves living in England for periods of, in some cases, up to five years.

There is no harder test for a volunteer army than a long period of inaction and frustration. It is quite possible that the future historian of the Canadian Army in this war will conclude that, of all its experiences, the long wait in England was in some respects the most severe trial of its discipline and morale.

At this comparatively late date, when the waiting is over and the Canadian Army is fully committed to action on two European fronts, it is possible to look at this question in some perspective. And it is hard to read the records without becoming increasingly convinced that this incident in the social history of the Empire is one which the two great parties to it—British and Canadian—have a right to regard with solid satisfaction. The maintenance of the morale of the Canadian troops at a high level during four years of enforced and unforeseen inaction, in a country which was not their own, and the maintenance of not merely good but steadily better relations with the people among whom they found themselves, is surely a great credit alike to the Canadian soldier and his British hosts.

GETTING TO KNOW EACH OTHER

The extraordinarily sound relationship which has been created between the Canadian Army Overseas and the people of Britain would have been worthy of note in any conditions. It becomes particularly significant, however, when one stops to consider that the two nations, while united by ancient and powerful bonds of sentiment and by allegiance to the same Crown, are nevertheless decidedly different peoples, living in different continents, pursuing separate and distinctive ways of life (to which each party is strongly wedded), and not even altogether the same in national origins—for the ancestors of a great many men of the Canadian Army did not come from the British Isles. There was thus a very considerable initial gap between hosts and guests; and the fact that this gap was bridged so successfully is a happy portent for the British Commonwealth and perhaps, even, for the world at large. The whole incident would have been less important if there had been no difficulties to overcome.

The Canadians, we have said, arrived in England during the period of the "phony war", when the Western Front was completely static, when enemy air attacks against the United Kingdom had not yet begun, and when, perhaps, the peril confronting the country was not yet fully apparent to the average Briton. It is well worth noting also that they arrived in the midst of a winter which brought to England "the coldest conditions since 1894"—a condition for which English barracks, or indeed any English buildings, were not designed, and which inevitably made the troops uncomfortable to a very high degree. Add to this the fact that the Canadian soldiers themselves were fresh from civil life and unaccustomed to army service and the degree of discomfort and privation inseparable from it, and it is clear that the relationship between them and the people of England was not inaugurated under ideal conditions.

The 1st Canadian Division spent its first winter in England in the barracks at Aldershot. Now Aldershot had been a great military centre since the Crimean War, and soldiers were very far indeed from being novelties there. The Canadians received much kindness and hospitality from the people of the town and district, but no garrison town of long standing has ever appeared particularly attractive in the eyes of young volunteer troops full of the hope of early action. In the special conditions obtaining in that freezing winter of 1939-40 Aldershot was not a comfortable place, and the new arrivals frequently and inevitably found themselves merely miserable. Boredom, homesickness, and what one acute observer called "a feeling of not being really needed", combined to produce something like an epidemic of grumbling. It seemed that the Canadians and their English hosts were not "getting off on the right foot".

In the light of later events, however, this gloomy winter appears merely as a period of adjustment, and as the prelude to much better things. A few months brought the lovely English spring; they brought also the end of the "phony war" and a new realization among Canadians and Britons alike of the true nature of the crisis. For the Canadians, moreover, the events of the spring and summer meant freer movement about England, a more extensive knowledge of the country, and the opportunity of seeing the English people at their very best.

One incident in particular still stands out in many men's memories of 1940. When in Dunkirk Week Canadian Force moved into the Northampton area, the troops were greeted as though they had been a liberating army; and the kindly warmth of the welcome gave them a new (and certainly more accurate) impression of England. The War Diary of one unit records:

"The local inhabitants greeted the battalion very kindly. Hot tea and cake was given to the men as they debussed and everyone was most friendly. The civilians were most hurt if troops were not billetted with them." Another noted that the hospitality of the good folk of Kettering was such that "meal parades were very small"; and still another wrote, when the time came to depart, "To say that we regretted leaving Northampton would be putting it mildly. The people took us to their hearts and their kindness and hospitality will be forever remembered by the Canadians." That very short stay in Northamptonshire did more than any previous episode to produce a warm relationship between the Canadians and their English hosts.

As the war went on, the morale of the troops and their relationship with the British people naturally had their ups and downs in keeping with the course of events. The winter of 1941-42 in particular was a rather difficult time, for reasons which are not far to seek. The enemy's air attacks on Britain, which had lent excitement to the previous winter, had now virtually ceased, and there was no longer the exhilarating sensation of being close to the front line. On the contrary, since the German attack on Russia in the summer of 1941 the Canadians had had the feeling of being in a backwater of the war; and their spirits were depressed accordingly. To make matters still worse, war had broken out in the Pacific in December; and two battalions sent from Canada met the Japanese at Hong Kong before any unit of the Canadian Army Overseas crossed bayonets with the Germans. In these circumstances, men who had been in the army well over two years—many had actually spent two years in the United Kingdom—felt that they had some right to feel gloomy, the more so as the shape of the war seemed to offer them no immediate prospect of action. In this "browned-off" mood they were not particularly good company for themselves or anybody else. This, however, proved to be only a passing phase. At no time since have such conditions recurred.

The simple basic fact is that, on balance, relations between the Canadian troops and the people of Britain have improved steadily since the first winter of the war, until today they are scarcely susceptible of further improvement. Any officer or soldier who has spent a long period in Britain will testify that this is the case; and there is very strong evidence in official files to prove it. Every scrap of this indicates that, while in the earlier days of the war the Canadians were not unanimous in their regard for the people among whom they were living, by 1944 the situation had wholly changed. The relations between British civilians and Canadian troops were now cordial in the last degree. There had been uncertainty and misunderstanding; now, there was understanding so complete that it could literally be called universal. The thing had become a matter of course.

It is interesting to speculate on the circumstances which have brought about this happy result. Much of the credit, undoubtedly, is due to the German Air Force, which by its attacks on England in 1940-41 and at various later periods placed the Canadians and the English people in a relationship similar to that of comrades in a theatre of war. The British civilian of 1939, so set in his ways, so very obstinately English, so disinclined to enthuse over the stranger within his gates, so apparently oblivious to the war, might not appear to the Canadian soldier's inexperienced and hasty eye an especially sympathetic or admirable character; but the same civilian under the bombs, carrying on his daily work unperturbed by the growing desolation around him, and if anything rather more cheerful and definitely more friendly as the result of his unwonted and unparalleled perils, was a figure for whom the same soldier could have nothing but admiration.

England is a country which it takes some time to get to know. Scotland, of course, is a rather different matter. There is a queer, rather indefinable, affinity between Scotland and Canada. The Canadians got on famously with Scots from the beginning, and it soon became a standing joke (exactly as in the last war) that when one of them got seven days' leave he immediately demanded a railway warrant for Edinburgh, Glasgow or Inverness. In the early days, it is certain, the Canadians were more at home in those places than in England; but as time passed and they knew England better they penetrated the Englishman's celebrated "reserve" and established with him a relationship not inferior to that with the Scot.

This has been due in great part to the extraordinarily generous kindness and hospitality, both public and private, which the English themselves, in their unobtrusive way, have offered to their visitors. The famous episode in Northampton was only a striking symbol of a general situation which seldom comes out into the open quite as frankly as it did in those Dunkirk days. Hospitality is a difficult thing in wartime England; food is short, households that once had servants now have none, and almost every individual has some preoccupation arising from the war to reduce the amount of leisure which he or she can devote to the amenities of life. In spite of all this, the English have contrived to be hospitable. Public-spirited organizations have done much; but more, perhaps, has been done by private individuals out of patriotism and the sheer kindness of their hearts. No single thing, perhaps, has done so much for understanding as the fact that innumerable Canadians have been taken into English households and become almost members of the family. Nothing means so much to a soldier as this; nothing has done so much to foster what a great Governor-General once called "sound and kindly feelings between Canada and the Mother Country."

It is clear, too, that an element in producing better spirits among the Canadians, and therefore better relations with the people among whom they lived, was the gradually increasing expectation of early action. There was good reason for hope for a chance at the enemy any time from the spring of 1942 onwards. That year brought the first battle, the raid on Dieppe. The next summer saw a Canadian Division fighting in the Mediterranean. As for the final step, for many months before the actual invasion no secret had been made of the fact that the Allies intended to land in North-West Europe at a comparatively early date. The Canadian troops still in Britain now felt quite certain that they would be in battle soon. Their spirits rose accordingly, and the problems encountered in the days of gloomy inactivity were proportionately reduced.

An American writer, in a widely circulated magazine, has suggested that the arrival of great numbers of Americans in the British Isles after 1941 actually operated as a force bringing Canadians and Englishmen together. The Englishman and the Canadian, forced into close association in the early days of the war, had been very much aware of their own differences; but when the Americans arrived, says this writer, "The British, to their consternation, discovered that while the Americans had all the peculiarities of the Canadians, only in twice the intensity, they were an entirely different breed of North Americans, with infinitely more complicated racial strains. And so for the last two years the Canadians have been trying to explain Americans to the British, and the British to the Americans whom they met in the pubs". Canadians and Englishmen alike were now made conscious of what they had in common rather than of their differences; and the Canadians of the army in England found themselves actually performing that role of interpreter between the two halves of the English-speaking world which editors and orators have been fond of attributing to Canada, but which has rarely been undertaken by her people in so literal a sense.

Due credit must be given to the Canadian agencies that have been at work to maintain the welfare and the spirit of the troops. The Canadian Chaplain Service has lived up to its high traditions of the last war, and the regimental Padre has maintained his fine position as the soldier's confidant and friend, and has been indefatigable in his labours for the material as well as the spiritual comfort of his charges. At the same time the Canadian Auxiliary Services, uniting and co-ordinating the patriotic efforts of four great voluntary organizations, the Canadian Y.M.C.A. Overseas, the Salvation Army Canadian War Services, the Knights of Columbus Canadian War Services and the Canadian Legion War Services, have followed the soldier wherever he has gone and have provided him with comforts and entertainment, often in conditions where it might have seemed that such service was impossible. These strictly Canadian influences have done their part, and that not a small one, in keeping the Canadian soldier happy during the years of inaction, and thereby contributing to the maintenace of good relations between him and his English neighbours.

Essentially, however, the basic reason for the steady improvement in the Anglo-Canadian relationship has certainly been simply the good sense and goodwill of both parties. On the third anniversary of the arrival of the 1st Division in Britain, General McNaughton, commenting on the problem of morale, said that the thing that had simplified it was the fact that "our men have good common sense": that they were not an army of adventurers, but an intelligent body of men who had crossed the ocean to serve a cause, and who realized that the cause might demand of them waiting as well as fighting. And because they were intelligent men they were also understanding men who as they grew increasingly accustomed to England and

English ways inevitably acquired a strong regard for the country and its people. The English on their side, have shown equal understanding; and those of them who have seen much of Canadians have certainly found their own outlook modified in some particulars by the contact.

A special and significant symbol of the relationship has been the number of marriages which have taken place. The actual total of Army marriages in the United Kingdom to 31 August 1944 was 19,269. The vast majority of these were between Canadian officers or soldiers and British women. It is interesting to note how the total grew as the Canadian force in England increased and the Canadians became more at home in the country. In 1940 there were 1222 marriages; in 1941 there were 3011, and in 1942 there were 4160. 1943 produced 5879 (including 1128 in the month of July alone), while the total for 1944, to the end of August, was 4979.

Of all the aspects of the Anglo-Canadian relationship in Britain, this is perhaps the one most likely to exercise definite influence upon the future relations of the Dominion and the Mother Country. It is going to bring to Canada after the war a very large number of English girls to find new homes there. Already, in fact, many English wives of Canadian soldiers, assisted by the Government, have crossed the Atlantic, and their number is increasing.

* * * *

A special word must be said of the Canadians' relations with the British armed forces. This has been in some respects a special problem. Groups of soldiers are inclined to be critical of one another, particularly under static conditions; they dwell on small points of difference and make much of matters which to a civilian eye appear unimportant. One such subject of argument was the discrepancy between the British rate of pay and the higher Canadian. This was in large measure equalized by the Canadian device of "deferred pay" by which fifty per cent of the pay of men with no dependents is held back to accumulate interest for them until the end of hostilities; the out-of-pocket expenses of a visitor are inevitably higher than those of a resident. With subsequent increases in British Army pay, and the arrival in the British Isles of hundreds of thousands of soldiers of the United States Army, the original discrepancies lost all significance.

In spite of such special problems, the Canadians have got on well with the British soldier, and as in the case of relations with civilians, they have got on steadily better as time passed. One matter of particular interest is the regard which Canadians have shown for British instructors. This appeared from the beginning of the war. Canadians are outspoken people, and soldiers who have attended courses in British schools have been known to be critical of various particulars; nevertheless, criticism of the *instruction* has been very rare. The almost unanimous opinion has been that the British officers and N.C.Os. employed in such establishments "know their stuff": they know what to teach and how to teach it. These British schools have made a great contribution to the efficiency of the Canadian Army.

With one section of the British forces Canadian units have had a very special relationship. This is the Home Guard, the new citizen army which was created overnight ("out of nothing", as a Canadian officer once admiringly said) in the great national emergency of 1940. The Canadians have had a great deal to do with the Home Guard; their units have helped to train it in many parts of the country; and they have shared responsibility with it in schemes of local defence, in which throughout it has played a most vital role.

There has been something about the Home Guard that has particularly appealed to the Canadian soldier. Perhaps he has sympathized the more with its problems in that, in very many instances, he himself, in the old days of peace, knew what it was to be a part-time soldier. But there has also, it would seem, been a deep, if inarticulate, conviction that the Home Guard stands in a special manner for what is most solid and admirable in Britain. It is an institution characterized by hard work, high public spirit, and no frills.

If England was what England seems,
An' not the England of our dreams,
But only putty, brass an' paint,
'Ow quick we'd drop 'er! But she ain't.

There was very little putty, brass and paint about the Home Guard; and the Canadians, no great lovers of those commodities, respected it accordingly.

With the Sussex Home Guard they have been on particularly good terms. In June of 1942 a fortnight was especially devoted by the 1st Canadian Corps to training the Home Guard and training with the Home Guard. It was a very successful, and for both parties a very enjoyable period. A senior Home Guard officer later described it in a letter to *The Times:*

> . . . The experiment, for allowing for the many and varied occupations in which individual Home Guards are engaged, it must be regarded as such, has been an undoubted and unqualified success, both in the value of the actual training itself and in the remarkably high percentage of attendance.
>
> How large a share of this success is due to the real co-operation given by the Canadians is well known to the Home Guard, and the wholehearted understanding which exists between the two Forces will have lasting effects, not only during such time as they may soldier together, but in the years of peace which lie before us . . .

> The best tribute to the Canadians is the fact that for the whole of this fortnight, including three week-ends at the height of the agricultural urgency, night after night, and sometimes all night, the Home Guard turned up voluntarily in strength to train and to learn, and to show that, old and young, they could stick it.
>
> Over a period of many months and particularly during our training fortnight, we in the Home Guard, both from the civil and military point of view, have grown to know the Canadian soldier intimately. We have had a full opportunity to judge his character individually and collectively, and we are honoured to accept him as a comrade in the truest sense of the word . . .

Out of this relationship grew a presentation to the Corps from the Home Guard of Sussex, which subscribed nearly £700 for the purpose. The Zone Commander (Colonel E. J. W. Pike) took up with General Crerar the question of the use to be made of the money. The Corps Commander was quite certain that all ranks of the Corps would wish that the fund should remain in Sussex and its benefits accrue to the Sussex Home Guard or to any military or semi-military organization that might in due course succeed it. Accordingly, a portion of the money was applied in the purchase of a trophy to be known as the Canadian Corps Trophy, while the income from the balance is to be utilized to provide annual prizes to the unit or sub-unit of the Sussex Home Guard that may be adjudged the most efficient.

General Crerar presented the Canadian Corps Trophy in a ceremony on 26 September 1943, only a short time before the balance of the Corps embarked for the Mediterranean. The Corps Commander in his address spoke of the strain to which the men of the Corps had been subjected as the result of "being held for these four years of war mainly on the side lines". The officers and men of the Corps, he said, could not have won this spiritual battle "if it had not been for the kindness, sympathy and understanding of the Sussex people amongst whom we had lived for these years". He concluded:

> Now, that is all I have to say, except to tell the people of Sussex, through those present, that because you have understood us and opened your homes to us and helped us, I can assure you that those of us who return to Canada will take with us the intention that the ties which have previously existed between this country and our own should be strengthened; that more effective means to co-operate in preventing a recurrence of wars should be mutually developed; and that, in the evolution of a better world order, the British Empire—tested and purified by the experience through which we are passing—will have a vital part to play.

The Canadian Corps Trophy, a permanent memorial of one of the very good things that have come out of a very bad period of history, may perhaps stand as a symbol of the whole relationship between the Canadian soldier and the people of England; and General Crerar's remarks provide an eloquent commentary upon that relationship and the permanent profit to mankind which, it may be hoped, will spring from the Canadians' long sojourn in Britain.

"SINGLE MEN IN BARRICKS"

Enough has been said to suggest what a severe test the discipline of the troops underwent during the long years in England. Now that that phase is over and the episode can be seen from a little distance, it is interesting to look at the actual record of the behaviour of these young Canadians far from home.

There were certain periods when, on the basis of reports and comments in the press, and particularly some of the more lurid journals, it might have appeared that the Canadians were actually an unusually badly behaved army. (There are especially unpleasant memories of a certain abusive letter in a Sussex newspaper, and much more agreeable ones of the sound verbal chastisement which the anonymous writer immediately received from Lord Winterton, the senior M.P. for Sussex). Now and then there were generalized strictures from the magisterial bench. At times, the Canadians might almost have felt disposed to expostulate with some of the critics in the words which Kipling put into the mouth of an English soldier of a much earlier day:

> We aren't no thin red 'eroes, nor we aren't
> no blackguards too,
> But single men in barricks, most remarkable
> like you.

That there were instances of bad behaviour by Canadian soldiers is of course true. A force of hundreds of thousands of men from any nation inevitably includes a certain number of black sheep, as well as a certain number of men whose mere high spirits will inevitably get them into trouble if conditions are right—or wrong. But that the number of black sheep was exceptionally large in the case of the Canadians is most certainly not true. The official figures indicate, on the contrary, that the number of offences has been rather surprisingly small in relation to the size of the Canadian force in the United Kingdom and the conditions under which it has served.

Of special interest is the fact that comparatively few Canadian soldiers have got into trouble with the civil authorities. A report prepared in 1942 states that down to the end of August of that year the total number of recorded civil convictions was only 923. It was admitted that these figures might not be quite complete, but they were accurate enough to establish the fact that the proportion of troops involved in civil prosecutions was distinctly small. Subsequently, further reports indicated that

HELPING WITH THE HARVEST
Canadian soldiers lend a hand on an English farm.

NO PRIVACY TO BE HAD
English children invade an office in the field.

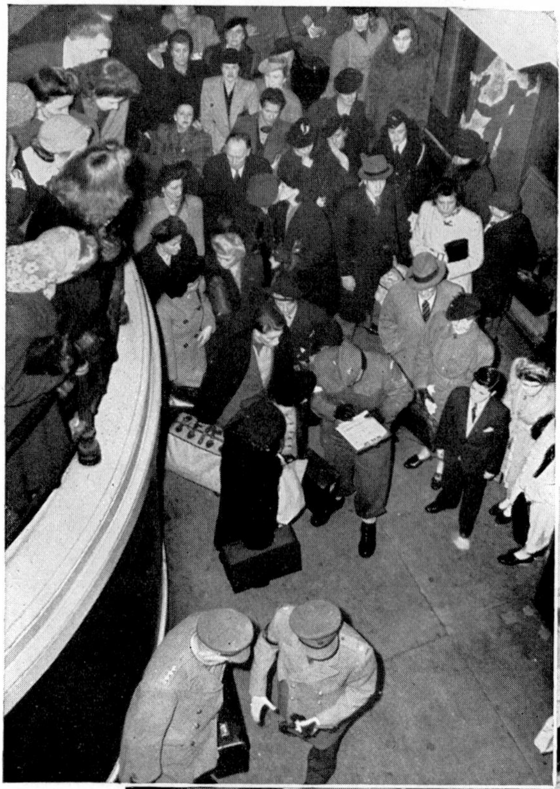

EUSTON STATION, LONDON, 1944

Wives of Canadian servicemen leaving for new homes in Canada.

CHRISTMAS, 1942

A children's party at a Canadian General Hospital in England.

the situation was improving rather than deteriorating. A report covering the discipline of the army during the last quarter of 1942 indicated that "approximately one-third of one per cent" of the troops had been convicted of civil offences during that period. A later report, dealing with the opening months of 1943, analyzed the relative statistics and concluded, "As an average figure, 4 to 5 soldiers out of every 10,000 are involved with the civil authorities each month". The situation thus described has remained fairly constant ever since. For example, during the three months ending 30 September 1943 there were 219 civil convictions of Canadian soldiers in the United Kingdom. This, out of a force of more than two hundred thousand men, is a record which compares very favourably with that of any civilian community.

These things are worth saying. The Canadians during these years of inaction faced the sort of situation in which the discipline of an army could easily go completely to pieces. This did not happen with them. In spite of all difficulties and temptations, their general conduct was a credit to their country; and at the end of the period their standard of discipline was higher than it had been at the beginning, and their relations with their English hosts were so friendly that they could scarcely have been bettered. This record is one upon which Canadians of later generations may look back with a certain pride.

A QUARTER OF A MILLION AMBASSADORS

This pamphlet has told a little—only a little—of the life and activities of the Canadian army in Britain during the years 1939-44. During those years a quarter of a million Canadian soldiers were guests of Britain, not under favourable conditions, but in the hard circumstances of wartime living and at a time when they would have greatly preferred to be fighting. They were simply very ordinary Canadians, a cross-section of the Dominion from Halifax to Victoria and from Lake Erie to the

Arctic. Nevertheless, they were ambassadors for the Dominion in the United Kingdom; and in the light of all that has been said it may perhaps be admitted now that their embassy was a successful one.

They crossed the Atlantic to fight for their country and the Commonwealth, and for the standards for which, in their minds, Canada and the Commonwealth stood. They were denied the chance of actual fighting for a long period. They knew that their time would come, and come it did. As these lines are written, the Canadian Army has long been fully committed to action in Italy and in North-West Europe. When the Canadian history of this war is written, it will doubtless be of victories in these regions that it will chiefly tell. In a sense, however, the Canadians' first victory was won not on the battlefield but in the British Isles. There they met and surmounted as severe a test of spirit as has been faced by any army in this generation. When at length they sailed from the United Kingdom for the theatres of war, they left behind them millions of English people whose knowledge of and regard for the Dominion of Canada were far greater than in 1939. This fact should be set down for the record.

In the years of reconstruction ahead, the British Commonwealth has a great part to play. It is for the Commonwealth, itself a working League of Nations and a practical example of the co-operation of all sorts and conditions of men from all over the world, to take the lead in bringing mankind back to sanity and goodwill. If it is to succeed in doing so, the Commonwealth must know itself; for in knowing itself it will, to no small extent, know and understand the world as well. To this increase of knowledge the Canadian sojourn in England during 1939-44 made no minor contribution. On two battle-fronts today the Canadians are doing much to win the war. Perhaps what they did during those years in England may ultimately make some contribution to winning the peace.

NOTICE . . .

This book is the first of a series to be published by the Government Printing Bureau on behalf of the Department of National Defence in 1945 and 1946.

Those to be published this year are:

No. 1

"THE CANADIANS IN BRITAIN, 1939-1944"

THE YEARS OF WAITING

Published in May, 1945

No. 2

"FROM PACHINO TO ORTONA"

THE CAMPAIGN IN SICILY AND ITALY, JULY-DECEMBER, 1943

To be published in July, 1945

No. 3

"FROM CAEN TO FALAISE"

THE NORMANDY CAMPAIGN, JUNE-AUGUST, 1944

To be published in October, 1945

Readers are urged to reserve copies of future issues from their bookseller or to order direct from The King's Printer, Ottawa, Ontario, enclosing Money Order or Postal Note to cover cost.

PAPERBOUND COPIES . . . 25c Each **CLOTHBOUND EDITION . . . 50c Each**

MOVEMENTS OF "CANADIAN FORCE"

SOUTH-EASTERN ENGLAND 1940

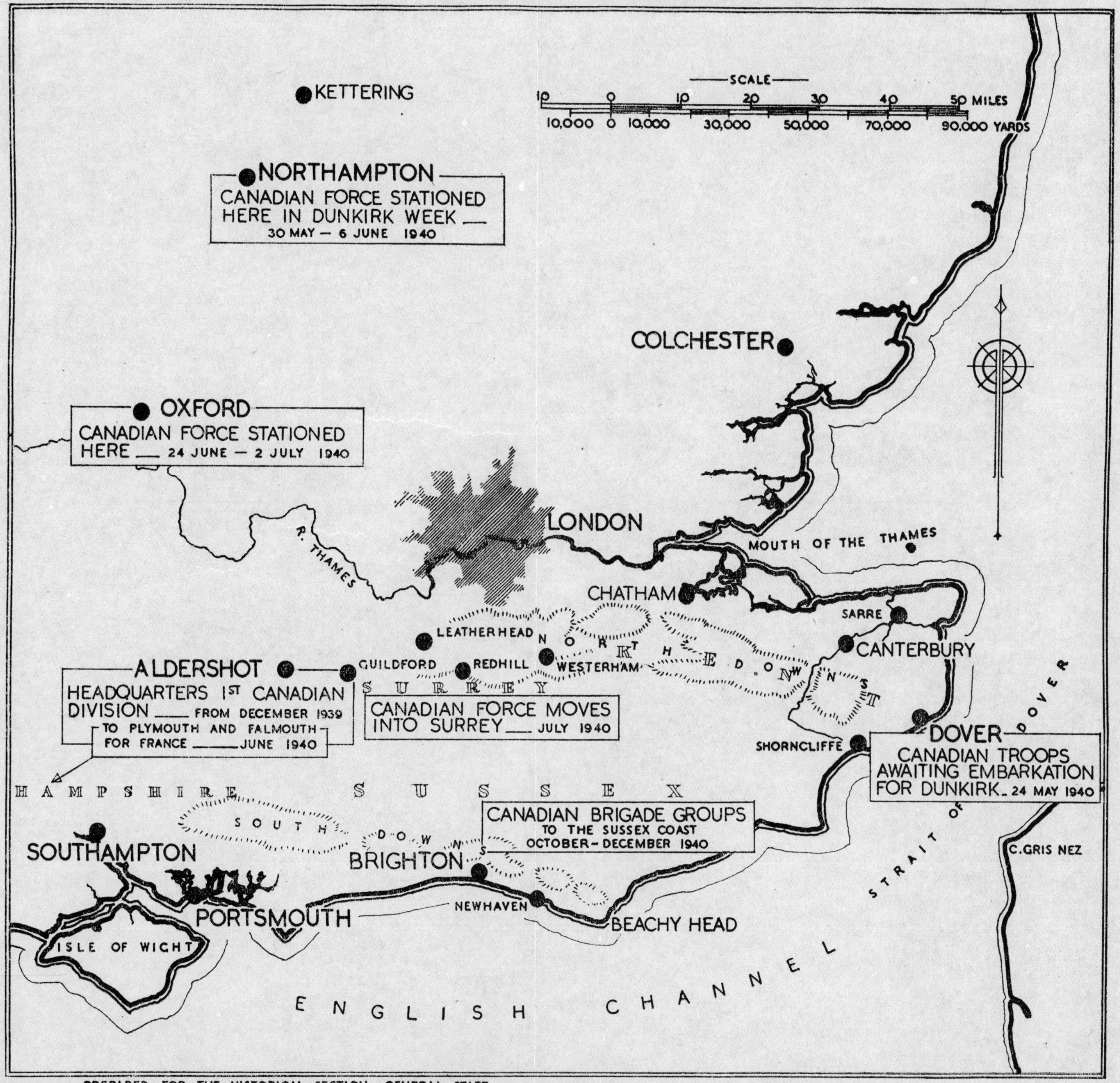

PREPARED FOR THE HISTORICAL SECTION, GENERAL STAFF,
CANADIAN MILITARY HEADQUARTERS, LONDON BY CPL. F. SHADLOCK, R.C.E.